Ultralight IT

Ultralight IT

Edited by Christine Niles
Cover image created by lauria at fiverr.com
Graphics produced by the Author using Canva
Additional photos from Wikimedia Commons

Gordium Publishing
info@ultralight.cloud

Ultralight IT

A Guide for Smaller Organizations

(Or: how I learned to stop worrying and love the cloud)

by ANDREW SCHWAB

Contents

SYN

ACK

Introduction

What is Ultralight?

In this book, Ultralight is shorthand for an idea that emerged over the past few years as my team and I faced a seemingly impossible task: provide great IT support using inexperienced staff with a tiny budget for a highly volatile organization that operated in more than 50 countries.

The conventional wisdom insisted we manage increasingly cumbersome onsite systems by adding yet more complexity and cost to our shop. Every vendor had something to sell, but no one could tell us how we were supposed to make it all fit together into a coherent whole with the time, money, and experience we actually had.

In truth, we didn't need more technology - we needed a way to *think* about technology that allowed us to identify, deploy, and maintain the right capabilities for our staff. In addition, we needed to be able to do it with the people and budget we actually had.

And we wanted it to be awesome.

Ultralight Defined

Ultralight is a framework for achieving excellence through simplicity. With Ultralight, small IT teams employ the latest cloud-based tools to increase capabilities while reducing management and maintenance overhead. This gives IT the freedom to focus on higher value activities such as providing an amazing user experience, making it easier to get work done, and supporting real business transformation.

To be successful, IT must get out from under the proverbial hood to focus on where the organization needs to go. The Internet becomes the only network that truly matters, empowering users to get work done from anywhere, on any device, at any time. IT's priorities transition from managing a cost center to generating real value.

Doing this requires a change in how the IT department thinks and functions. Ultralight lays out a pathway to transform the IT department into a value-driven team of business enablers. The IT team must be focused on business goals, applying their expertise where it can have the biggest impact in the organization. This means less time fiddling with servers and more time collaborating with business leaders and educating users.

Ultralight views security comprehensively, prioritizing what will make organizations most resilient. The old approach demanded that every organization reinvent the wheel even as the cart was bouncing down the road. Ultralight lets the world's leading experts provide baseline security and focuses instead on gaining visibility and control in the organization.

To be clear, Ultralight isn't an instant fix for all the problems IT faces. Rather, it is a framework for finding answers.

Who is this book for?

This book is for the person making IT decisions in a *small and medium business* (SMB) environment. I wrote this book because I couldn't find it when I needed it. When I went looking, I was able to find two kinds of technology books:

1. Books on high-level IT strategy for large organizations

2. Books with step-by-step instructions for doing the things large organizations want to do

Neither were very helpful, because neither spoke to the challenges I was actually facing. To do things the big-business way requires a critical mass of skills, resources, and structure. The organization I was a part of lacked this critical mass. And I don't think I was alone.

When the same IT person (or small team) must simultaneously put out fires and attempt to implement strategy, it is strategy that falls to the wayside. This results in more firefighting and less planning, which leads to more fires, and on it goes. What I needed was a practical guide for making decisions, and a path to *reach* critical mass.

This book describes a way to narrow the technological divide between big and small organizations, to lower the threshold to reach the critical mass essential to great IT integration and support. It is a bootstrapping process. As such, it proposes solutions geared specifically towards organizations with 500 or fewer users.

The recommendations that follow are compromises between manageability, accessibility, security, and cost. Each organization will weigh the relative importance of these factors differently, but the principles should prove instructive either way. My hope is that the Ultralight principles help bring simplicity, excellence, and value to your organization.

Using this Book

This book is broken down into three sections.

It is important to understand from the outset that the author is a nerd. The first section, **Better Things**, is my attempt to put Ultralight into words relevant for business-minded people. My hope is to explain how it can empower your organization as a whole with as little technical jargon as possible.

This first section also explains why I wrote this book and the circumstances that inspired Ultralight. It explores the management practices necessary to build an amazing IT team even if you're not the hippest, richest employer in town. And it stares down the barrel of the cyber-security threat and argues for the cloud as the best protection.

The second section, **Understanding Ultralight**, is a guide for technology decision makers. It focuses on deployment strategies and considerations. I've aspired to be as platform-agnostic as possible in this section, with an emphasis on broad applications for the Ultralight principles.

Finally, **Deploying Ultralight** walks through specific deployment considerations for an Ultralight organization built around Google Apps. Google Apps is not the only platform available to build an Ultralight organization, but it is has two key merits for the purpose of this book. First, in a very young field, it has some of the greatest depth and history. Second, it is the one I've personally deployed and can speak to.

I'd also like to take a moment here to define what I mean when I refer to IT, or the IT department. Unless specifically stated otherwise, I'm referring to *operational IT*: the team that manages an organization's *internal* technologies. If you have a back-office full of coders doing client work, that's great! Ultralight can help the operational IT team better support them. But the principles, techniques, and technologies in this book focus primarily on improving infrastructure and operations.

Finally, Ultralight provides a reference for decision making. It addresses the *why* and the *big how* when implementing technologies. The *small how* - the step-by-step guides for deploying individual tools - are all available online and likely to change week by week. I won't waste your time with them here.

The Value of IT Excellence

It is important that we deploy technology well. Doing so enables the organizations we support to achieve real, measurable, and lasting value. It can even be the difference between success and failure.

Great IT gives an organization's staff the confidence to focus on what matters most and the tools to do it well. Conversely, any loss of access to an important resource, inopportune program crash, or mid-day network outage disrupts the flow vital to real productivity. When technology fails, how much time does a critical team lose? What opportunities are lost? What is the real cost of poorly implemented and supported technology?

In a study looking at 60 different companies, Jeff Rumburg from MetricNet explored these questions by examining the impact of IT support on employee productivity. His research measured the average time employees sat around idly waiting for support when something was broken. He found that organizations with the best IT support **reduced lost productivity by up to two-thirds**. Not surprisingly, users working with a best-run shop were measurably happier too.

> *"The majority of today's workforce is comprised of knowledge workers, all of whom rely upon one or more computing devices to do their jobs. When these devices break down or do not function properly, employee productivity suffers. By preventing these incidents from occurring, and by quickly resolving issues when they do occur, a support organization can return productive hours to the workforce."*[1]

[1] https://www.metricnet.com/it-support-value-proposition/

While Rumburg's observation speaks specifically to the IT service desk, the value of excellent IT goes much further. Reduced system downtime, improved connectivity, faster access, higher quality tools, simpler software platforms, more fluid deployments, better educated employees, and engaged IT staff can combine to make IT a tremendous value generator. Understanding this, our question becomes: how does a real-world IT department achieve this kind of value generation? This is what my team and I needed to answer, and what inspired our journey towards Ultralight.

Introduction

Part 1: Better Things

We have better things to do than fight with technology. Unfortunately the traditional approach to supporting technology in our organizations has been expensive, time consuming, inflexible, and insecure. This is true for large and small organizations, though the challenge is particularly acute for smaller businesses and nonprofits.

The rise of cloud technologies promised to solve these problems but the marketing claims have largely rung hollow. The industry solution to the toils of managing a classic datacenter has been to replace it with a custom hybrid-cloud hyper-converged distributed datacenter. Organizations are left with the cost, complexities, and risk of their old technology, plus the additional cost, complexities, and risk of their cloud platform.

Ultralight is an alternative response to this challenge, a strategy for employing technology with excellence that focuses on doing fewer things, but doing them really well. Ultralight is grounded in brutal honesty about what organizations *need* technologically, what they *can actually do*, and what they *must do well* to succeed.

Before we can go any further, however, we need to take a hard look at how we got where we are today.

An Honest Assessment

We live in the real world, with constraints on our time and resources. We work for organizations where technology is a means to the end, not the end itself. We have IT teams made of real people, and budgets that limit what we can do and who we can hire.

This creates a number of business challenges.

We are Masters of None (The Scope Problem)

Every organization today must be able to communicate and collaborate electronically. This is true whether we have five employees or 50,000. We all need electronic messaging, a straightforward way to share information, mobile communication, and protection from theft or loss. While implementations vary, the *scope* of IT requirements is largely the same no matter where we are.

This creates a huge problem for small organizations. Implementing all these things requires us to manage a deep stack of technology: physical networks, servers, firewalls, operating systems, application configurations, cross-platform integration, virtualization, service providers, authentication, high availability, backups, and so on.

A large organization has the *scale* to hire experts in each technical area, a scale that smaller organizations lack. Small organizations may have a one-person shop or a few IT gurus patching together technology as best they can. In this kind of environment, trying to emulate traditional best practices is infeasible. What works best for the big guys simply doesn't scale down for the average business owner.

Great tech implementation requires a deep understanding of how everything fits together. But technology changes too quickly for a jack-of-all-trades shop to develop that deep understanding. Best practices are constantly evolving, implementations are too complex, the cost for expertise is too high, and every new innovation compounds the challenge.

Most proposed solutions to this problem involve buying *more* technology to help better manage what we already have. For large organizations with a deep cadre of experts, these *tech-for-your-tech* solutions may save time and money by increasing their ability to scale efficiently.

For smaller organizations, the problem is still scope: there are too many different *types* of problems to solve and not enough expertise in each domain. *Tech-for-your-tech* solutions simply add to the list of tools organizations must deploy. As that deployment list grows, they're done incompletely, insecurely, and ineffectively.

In small organizations, no matter how an IT team slices the time, there isn't enough expertise to go around. This cascades into a wide array of dysfunctions that hurt the business.

Our Security is Terrible

In truth, this isn't just a small organization problem. Large organizations, even when they have the scale necessary to hire experts and deploy best practices, still struggle to implement and secure tech effectively. The complexities of managing IT from the ground up is daunting even for the well-resourced.

A recent NSA disclosure detailed more than 600 corporate, private, or government organizations that had been successfully hacked by the Chinese[2]. The past few years have seen a string of high-profile attacks targeting companies including Sony, Target, J.P. Morgan, the US Office of Personnel Management, and the IRS. IT security failures have cost senior executives their jobs, damaged the reputations of strong brands, and cost an estimated $445 billion annually in the United States.[3]

This is not because the challenge is new or unexpected. Back in 2000, Microsoft security expert Butler W. Lampson observed, "After thirty years of work on computer security, why are almost all the systems in service today extremely vulnerable to attack? The main reason is that **security is expensive to set up and a nuisance to run,** so people judge from experience how little of it they can get away with."[4]

This remains true for organizations today. As individuals and organizations become ever more connected, the risk of catastrophic loss and the challenge of effectively securing data continues to grow.

---

[2]http://www.nbcnews.com/news/us-news/exclusive-secret-nsa-map-shows-china-cyber-attacks-us-targets-n401211

[3]http://www.mcafee.com/us/resources/reports/rp-economic-impact-cybercrime2-summary.pdf

[4]Emphasis added, http://www.acsac.org/invited-essay/essays/2000-lampson.pdf

We Can't Afford Amazing IT Staff

It's a good time to be a skilled information technology worker. As job opportunities have grown, so have paychecks and incentives. Computerworld's 2015 IT Salary Survey showed salaries steadily increasing, with the rate of increase accelerating into 2015.[5]

This is making it increasingly difficult to hire and retain IT staff. Those you need most, the ones with specialized skills, typically demand the greatest premiums.[6] And as job opportunities continue to grow, so do the incentives for experienced IT staff to move on.

The most influential factor in IT job hopping is increased pay. Skilled professionals can expect a 15% to 20% pay increase by jumping ship. While these challenges are most acute in specialized fields like information security (exacerbating the challenge described previously), increased hiring demand is present across the spectrum of technology-related jobs.

In the enterprise, 25% of projects are abandoned due to personnel shortages and one-third of total personnel recruiting budgets are spent acquiring IT talent. In this high-demand environment, many IT professionals have discovered they can do without a single employer, negotiating for the pay and lifestyle they want on the freelance market.[7]

---

[5]http://www.computerworld.com/article/2909514/salarysurvey2015/it-salaries-2015-cash-is-back.html

[6]http://www.computerworld.com/article/2909559/salarysurvey2015/in-hot-jobs-market-it-workers-call-the-shots.html

[7]http://www.cio.com/article/2982976/there-still-arent-enough-tech-workers-and-enterprises-are-paying-the-price.html

Smaller, non-technology organizations must compete not only against bigger pay, but bigger brands and bigger ambitions. Joe's Workshop may legitimately make the best hand-crafted wood furniture available, but, even at comparable pay, Joe may struggle to hire top technology talent. The best IT minds will look to where they can have the greatest impact in their field: places like Silicon Valley.

Google, Microsoft, Amazon, and other large technology companies offer not just pay and benefits, but the opportunity to work with some of the greatest technology leaders in the world. For an expert technologist, these companies offer incredible development opportunity and career potential.

For technologists with both high aptitude and high risk tolerance, ambitious tech startups offer autonomy and the possibility to inspire the future - plus the chance to become phenomenally wealthy. Focused startups may target rising stars right out of high school or college, before they ever venture into the formal job market.

But Joe's Workshop still needs technology to market and manage their business, which means they'll make do with what they can find. Many times this can mean less knowledgeable or less experienced staff.

Which leads to our next problem.

In-house Tech is Horrible and Expensive

Uncle Jimmy is a great guy. He is trustworthy, conscientious, and dedicated to the business. What he isn't is a technology pioneer. To support technology at Joe's Workshop, Jimmy relies on outside experts he believes have the knowledge to help. However, those experts aren't altruists - they're sales people, and their job is to get paid.

The question isn't whether they'll provide Uncle Jimmy with something that can do the job. They certainly will. The question is how much it will cost the organization, and whether or not the organization can sustainably support it.

It is critical to understand that the real cost of a technology is in *operation*, not purchase. It is the complexity of a technology, not the initial capital investment, which determine its long-term opportunity cost. This goes back to the scope problem: it's no use having the "best" technology in the world if the IT team can't afford to implement it fully and maintain it well.

This is doubly true when initial costs are heavily discounted. For non-profits, organizations like TechSoup make it possible to purchase hardware and software at substantial discounts. Unfortunately, these savings can distract from the real cost of implementing, operating, and maintaining a set of technologies.

At one organization, I arrived shortly after the purchase of a completely new datacenter platform. This platform was incredibly capable. It could easily have scaled to many times our current requirements, and it actually cost less for the initial purchase than a more traditional platform.

The problem was, while it was tremendously powerful, it was also complex far beyond our needs. While we didn't need all that scaling power, we still had to manage the inherent complexity. To certify our team to fully understand the equipment's capabilities was going to take 18 months and cost *nearly as much as the hardware itself.* The hardware wasn't poor - it was fantastic. But the added complexity brought with it a plethora of hidden costs and new distractions. Having *more* than we needed was nearly as bad as *not having enough*: we were still left struggling to provide effective support.

Finally, relying on value-added resellers (VARs) or managed service providers (MSPs) to fill the gap is no protection from this problem. They have tremendous incentive to introduce the maximum level of complexity into an environment. Their ultimate goal is driving growth for their business. They understand that, particularly for smaller and less experienced IT shops, increased complexity is synonymous with increased dependence on their services.

The Personal Computer is Dead

The mainframes of the 1950s were large, expensive, slow, and challenging to maintain. They were the *First Platform.* These costly, room-filling computing machines made incredible things possible, but their use was limited to organizations with the resources required to own and operate them. Their direct integration with smaller businesses was minimal - a typewriter was a much more accessible tool.

Thankfully, during the 1960s and 70s, improvements in manufacturing and integrated circuit design made digital components smaller, faster, and cheaper. The *Second Platform*, the personal computer, came into its own in 1977 with the release of multiple mass-market PC designs including the Apple II.

Unlike mainframes, PCs came to us, and many more businesses could afford to purchase and operate them. PCs were small and cheap, allowing anyone to crunch data right at their desk. Local networking connected users around the office, driving information sharing, collaboration, and productivity. The *Second Platform* became a core part of how businesses, large and small, got work done.

The problem was that, while inexpensive, personal computers brought tremendous complexity into business environments. Users had to learn new skills. Hardware had to be researched, purchased, secured, integrated, tracked, and disposed of. Software had to be licensed, configured, patched, updated, and eventually replaced. Networks had to be built, secured, upgraded, and inevitably rebuilt. And every component interacted with every other component in curious and unexpected ways, with *unexpected* occasionally culminating in *catastrophic*.

The explosion of the Internet in the 1990s, the birth of mobile communication, and the rise of cloud-based applications added layer upon layer of complexity to the *Second Platform*. Today, many organizations are still fighting to fit each new innovation into *Second Platform* thinking - a technology mindset that is nearly 40 years old.

Yet, even as new technologies encumbered the Second Platform, they've made a whole new approach possible. This new approach is built on the *Third Platform*, which shifts the focus from hardware to services and from local networks to the Internet. Specific devices matter less as we focus on the capabilities they connect us to. With the Third Platform, our critical information can be available anywhere, at any time, on any device.

The personal computer is dead, and this should be a good thing. If we're willing to consider it, the Third Platform can provide real answers to the challenges we've just explored. Ultralight is a way to move past the Second Platform once and for all, and start thinking in terms of the Third Platform and the power and simplicity it can bring.

Ultralight Objectives

Move from:	To:
Complex	Simple
System oriented	People oriented
Cost driven	Value driven
Reactive	Proactive

The Ultralight Organization

In Jim Collin's book <u>Good to Great</u>, he explores key concepts an organization must master to transition from mediocre to excellent. The concepts start with providing great leadership and building the right team, then move to disciplined thought, and culminate with disciplined action. The very last step, *technology accelerators*, addresses how to use technology to build on positive momentum.

Technology integration matters, but it is the *last* concept to be applied in building a great organization. This placement is crucial and in direct contrast to how we're too often conditioned to think about technology.

We live in an age of incessant marketing, and no slogan is forced upon us more actively than this: *technology will solve your problem.* We see this most directly in the "there's an app for that" culture, and it's a great way to sell people junk. Vendors want us to believe every business problem can be fixed with a new technology product.

It can't. Technology can enable a team in remarkable ways, but it cannot stand in the place of the vital qualities the team must possess to be successful. Whenever technology is deployed to compensate for what is fundamentally a people problem, it can only obscure and complicate the dysfunction.

It is people that cast vision, build motivated teams, identify root problems, and exercise competence and resolve. To achieve success, the IT department must view all technology decisions through the lens of enabling and empowering the staff.

Each of the four Ultralight principles are grounded in this truth. Stated simply:

People, not technology, make an organization successful.

This is not a neo-luddite position. To the contrary, we must transform business processes to take advantage of the latest technologies. The key point here is precedence: people come first. Only when we've put people first will we understand how technologies can best enable their success.

Tom Goodwin of Havas writes, "[I]t's about people and behavior more than technology."[8] He goes on to clarify that making it about people will likely demand process change. We must retool how our businesses function to take advantage of the latest technology, giving staff the resources to excel.

---

[8]https://www.linkedin.com/pulse/3-big-trends-2016-tom-goodwin

"We should not just be adding new technology to our processes, we should be rebuilding processes around technology. We should be seeking to give all staff iPads and make their jobs and processes such that they don't need to use advanced PC's. Excel should be replaced by real time dashboards, presentations should be based on sharing information, not PowerPoint slides."

If we hope to accomplish this, there is no time for the IT department to hide in the server closet. The IT team must be engaged in the business and acutely aware of what users need to achieve success. Only then can they understand how best to integrate emerging technologies. Likewise, training and educating should be core competencies for IT staff, and a base level of business acumen should be considered essential for every IT staff member.

This isn't the default state for most IT shops, which means a culture shift is required. The first two principles of Ultralight, *excellence-focused* and *user-centered*, address this culture shift: how to think about problems, ask the right questions, and truly make people the priority. The two remaining principles, *cloud-based* and *hardware-minimizing*, provide a framework for how to actually make this happen.

The 4 Ultralight Principles

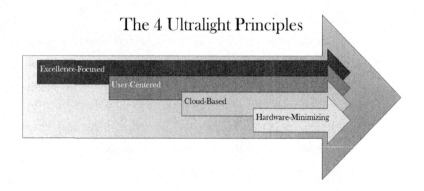

Excellence-Focused

User-Centered

Cloud-Based

Hardware-Minimizing

The Excellence-Focused Principle

Excellence-Focused:
Do in-house what you alone can do with excellence.
Eliminate or outsource the rest.

There are a few things *only* the IT team can do to bring excellence to an organization. Let them do those things. It won't be running a datacenter or building a distributed collaboration platform. Amazon and Google are better at it - period.

What Amazon, Google, and all the rest can't know is how to actually integrate technology to accomplish the organization's unique purpose. Only the IT team can bridge this divide between people and technology in the organization. The IT team must become experts on what staff really need to be productive. And to create space to become experts, IT must remove unnecessary complexity from the local environment. Basically, if someone else can do it better, let them.

This approach to excellence is not new, it merely reaffirms a classic business principle. "If it isn't a differentiator, get it out of your house", writes Martha Heller in <u>The CIO Paradox</u>. Exploring *The Operations versus Strategy Paradox*, Heller examines how to become strategic with technology when every minute could be spent just keeping the wheels turning. To break the paradox, she recommends focusing on the elements of IT that are core to the business and getting rid of the rest.

Likewise, focusing on establishing and pursuing a few *wildly important goals* is the first discipline from Stephen Covey's <u>The 4 Disciplines of Execution</u>. Covey's wildly important goals are the things that actually accomplish the organization's vision and purpose. The enemy of these goals is what Covey calls the "whirlwind" - the constant stream of stuff that floods inboxes and keeps staff distracted from actually moving forward. It isn't enough to know what is important. The organization must be able to execute on that knowledge. Covey argues we must discipline ourselves against the whirlwind, against distraction, if we want to succeed.

Entrepreneur and angel investor Dharmesh Shah, founder of HubSpot, boils it down to a four word strategy: **do fewer things, better**.[9]

Excellence-focused is the opposite of survival-focused. A survival-focused IT team is forever putting out fires at the expense of truly strengthening the business. Absent deliberate effort, survival-focused is the natural state for the IT department. It is inevitable.

---

[9]http://onstartups.com/do-fewer-things-better

VERSUS

EXCELLENCE   SURVIVAL
FOCUSED

Measure **value**   Measure **cost**

Prefer high
performance   Prefer local
control

Focus on
understanding
users   Focus on
understanding
systems

Identify how users
will **succeed**   Identify how users
will **conform**

Address
root causes   Default to
break / fix

Explore new
approaches   **React** to new
requirements

Integrate web-
based capabilities   **Maintain** siloed
product stacks

As the scope problem increases, IT becomes overwhelmed and reactionary. New technologies and uneducated users cease to be opportunities and become enemies.

The excellence-focused principle turns this around and focuses on creating space to do the most important things really well, starting with empowering people.

The User-Centered Principle

User-Centered:
Empowering people is your first technology priority.
New technology should simplify your user's digital life.

People are an organization's most valuable resource, and technology deployments must reflect this. Technology should, first and foremost, better enable employees to focus on their big goals.

For this to happen, the IT team must have a great relationship with the rest of the organization. They should provide an amazing user experience with a focus on educating and equipping staff to be as productive as possible. Many times, this means IT's relationship with staff must do a 180, transitioning from adversarial to empowering. This relational transformation is the most critical element of the user-centered principle. Without it, IT will struggle to extract full value from even the best technologies.

VERSUS

USER   SYSTEM

CENTERED

Single login
for everything

Separate logins
for many systems

Productive from
any device

Productive only
on **single device**

Productive from
anywhere

Productive only
with **local network**

One data set
across apps

Redundant data
across toolsets

Voice integrated
across devices

Voice limited
to specific hardware

IT preserves
all user data

Users backup
their own data

Unplanned
outages are rare
and users report
them

Unplanned
outages are common
and users ignore them

The user-centered principle changes how technology decisions are made. In the simplest terms, a user-centered technology platform should enable users to easily communicate and collaborate from anywhere, on any device, all the time. This is the opposite of system-centered, where the IT team spends the bulk of their time managing complex infrastructure and enforcing user controls.

Historically, providing access to systems and data from any device required enormous investment and considerable technical expertise. Even when this was achieved, it was not typically very simple, secure or user friendly. Ultralight resolves these disparate goals, achieving simplicity and excellence by moving core tech capabilities to the cloud.

The Cloud-Based Principle

Cloud-Based:
Use a unified cloud solution for all core services.
Push all end-user systems to the cloud.

Ultralight is completely cloud-based, building on Google Apps for Work or Microsoft Office 365 for all core communication and collaboration. Additional services should mesh seamlessly and with minimal management overhead. No critical end-user capability should be bound to the local network.

It isn't controversial to insist on excellence, or empowering employees. But relying on the cloud is still, for many, a vexing proposition. With regard to the cloud, this book embraces two key realities:

1. The cloud is here to stay
2. The cloud is the best chance most small organizations have to achieve technology excellence

Reality #1: The cloud is here to stay

Studies by BetterCloud show that, in 2015, enterprise organizations ran an average of 18 cloud applications, and that number is expected to triple by 2017. More strikingly, 62% of organizations polled indicated they would be running 100% of their IT in the cloud by 2020.

BetterCloud observes, "Today, 12% of organizations surveyed run 100% of their IT in the cloud; in five years more than 50% of our respondents said they will be moving their IT entirely to the cloud; in 10 years, that number will climb past 70%."[10]

> "We are at the beginning of the biggest shift in IT in more than 20 years. The growing use of cloud office systems and the increasing reliance on cloud applications is driving us to a tipping point—an entirely new way of working.
>
> Cloud office systems are the foundation of the transition to the cloud, serving as the gateway to overall cloud adoption. Running 100% of IT in the cloud was unthinkable only a few

---

[10]http://blog.bettercloud.com/cloud-office-systems-adoption/

years ago, but as our data shows, in less than 10 years it will be the norm."

The question isn't **if** anymore, but **when** and **how**.

The transition is understandable. The cloud provides simplicity and capability on a scale inaccessible to most organizations on their own. To put things in perspective, one rough estimate from 2014 put Amazon's cloud platform at between 2.8 and 5.6 *million* servers, spread out across 87 datacenters in 28 availability zones. The author of the report states, "*Over the long haul, Amazon believes the massive scale of the public cloud will mean that very few organizations will run their own datacenters.*"[11]

In a broader context, this isn't as remarkable as it sounds. Rather, this is just another step in our growing economic interdependence. We don't typically build our own furniture, or sew our own clothes. Since the industrial revolution, specialization and division of labor have made it possible to mass produce countless products efficiently and to a high standard. When we need a car, we buy instead of build because it simply isn't worth our time and effort to reinvent what someone else has already efficiently mastered.

Interdependence enables excellence and economy, and this truth is reaching the digital services space. We're empowered like never before to eliminate distractions and focus on *our* mission. The time is rapidly approaching when building an in-house datacenter may be akin to

---

[11]http://www.enterprisetech.com/2014/11/14/rare-peek-massive-scale-aws/

assembling our own vehicle. There will be special uses cases where it is beneficial, but more and more businesses will find it unnecessary.

Reality #2: The cloud as the best chance

As Shah said, *do fewer things, better.* Heller insists we *focus on the core by removing the context.* Covey's 1st Discipline is to *identify wildly important goals and mitigate the whirlwind.* The cloud lets IT do this. Moving to the cloud allows IT to focus on what matters most to the organization, providing the technological foundation for business excellence.

Cloud-based solutions eliminate the need for local servers and complex local networking. With reduced infrastructure, the IT team can spend more time mastering capabilities the business really needs. This also makes it possible to run a great shop with less raw technology experience, and allows IT to focus their security efforts on the highest value tasks.

Efficiency-gains and cost-savings tend to be the best understood benefits of cloud computing, and it can certainly be encouraging to see the return-on-investment math. But outsourcing or centrally hosting services is only a stepping stone. With Ultralight, the focus is on empowering users, and that takes more than just offsite hosting.

When accessing data and services through the cloud, the focus should become *who you are,* not where you are or what system you're using. It is a shift from *systems* to *people.* Give each user a single digital identity that works across all the user's required resources. This single digital identity is the lynchpin of a unified user experience, and greatly improves IT's ability to analyze behavior and improve security.

To achieve this level of access, simplicity, security, and quality with onsite systems and services is, for most organizations, impossible. A small IT team can't be expert in every technology subdomain required to run each stack well. Too much time is burned on maintenance and system support, while too little is invested on robust integration and improving user workflows. It is difficult to create a smooth user experience from disaggregated systems, and impossible to track user behavior holistically across siloed platforms.

Properly deployed, the cloud makes it possible to achieve these goals by leveraging integrated, highly scalable services from the world's leading technology minds. Simply stated, this is the best chance most organizations have to provide a truly amazing technology experience for their workforce.

Building out an Ultralight platform with cloud-based infrastructure and a single digital identity is only half the battle, however. The other is to greatly simplify what IT must do to connect users to the resources they need.

The Hardware-Minimizing Principle

Hardware-Minimizing:
Treat all tech equipment as simply a gateway to the cloud.
Eliminate dependence on proprietary hardware
and custom configurations.

The IT team should be focused first on empowering people, then on integrating cloud-based capabilities, and lastly on configuring and managing hardware. The less they mess with hardware, the more time they have to do the important things.

This is the opposite of hardware-dependent. Individualized, highly-customized hardware is the enemy. Commoditize hardware everywhere it touches the environment. Identify the minimum configuration necessary to be successful (and secure), then move on. This is as true of notebooks and mobile devices as it is of servers and switches.

This principle focuses on liberation from vendor-specific hardware, operating system lock-in, and complex virtualization. The goal is to eliminate local servers wherever possible. As a general rule, end users should never interact with a local server. If the Internet is the primary network and the cloud handles core applications, there should be very few tasks left to support locally. It is the time saved here that makes everything else possible.

Reducing dependence on specific hardware also greatly simplifies how IT supports users' personal devices. It shouldn't matter whether users prefer Windows or macOS, a notebook or a tablet. They should be free to use what makes them most productive, and IT should be able to support them effectively.

Over the past decade, multiple device management tools have been developed that provide robust security and configuration controls without the need for complex onsite directories. Many of these tools work cross-platform and will support macOS, Windows, and mobile platforms through a single management interface. Leverage these tools to provide a consistent experience and solid security without hindering users or complicating hardware management.

Maximizing People

Moving to the cloud and reducing hardware complexity creates space for IT to be very intentional about how it supports and develops people.

To be successful, however, the process must start at home. IT must be able to develop its own talent effectively. The next section addresses how to build a strong IT team, a team that can go out and teach, advise, and collaborate with employees across the organization.

Turning Willing Into Able

Supporting technology well requires a strong team. Building that team is both critical and difficult. And the challenge is bigger than just handling the scope problem. Demand for quality tech staff is growing and many other organizations are hunting for the same skills you are.

In the tech industry, it is common to talk about highly selective hiring processes: only get the best of the best. In How Google Works, Eric Schmidt and Jonathan Rosenberg explain, "Smart coaches know that no amount of strategy can substitute for talent, and that is as true in business as it is on the field... For a manager, the right answer to the question 'What is the single most important thing you do at work?' is *hiring*."

According to Schmidt and Rosenberg, smart coaches "draft, recruit, or trade for the best players they can." And that is the rub. The odds are good most of us can't draft, recruit or trade like Google. While the recommendations in their book are fantastic business guidance, they focus heavily on *finding the most **Able**, and ensuring the able stay **Willing***.

If you can hire this way, great! But most small organizations can't, which means we need a different approach. Like the Oakland Athletics in Moneyball, recruiting by the Yankees' rules isn't going to work if we want to be the best we can be with the limited resources we have. Instead, we must learn to *turn new hires that are **Willing** into experts that are **Able***. Which means, while hiring is important, the most critical thing managers will do is *develop*.

This isn't a revolutionary idea. In the United States Army, everyone starts out young and inexperienced, working their way up from the bottom. The Army doesn't hire from the outside to fill middle and senior-level roles. If the Army wants competent leaders and technical experts, it can't poach them from other organizations. It has to develop them from the inside. It has to turn the *willing* it has into the *able* it needs.

Family-run businesses, nonprofits, the military, and many other organizations face some form of this same challenge. Location, compensation, affiliation, accession pathways, and a number of other factors limit the pool of candidates they can hire. A religious organization, for instance, will likely have a very willing pool of candidates - those that are aligned with the organization's values. But this group may be only a small subset of the total job seeker pool.

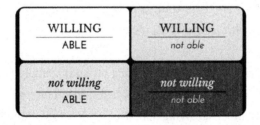

Hiring for Ultralight

Using the **Willing** *to* **Able** approach, four key elements make it possible to build a strong technology team regardless of the hiring pool:

1.   Hire first for a **willing attitude**. If you can only use one measure, make willingness to try the focal point of the initial hire. *Do they want to grow?*

2.   Validate a deep **learning capacity** through a provisional employment period. The key here is to identify who has the capacity for high performance. *Are they able to grow?*

3.   Initiate **long-term development** pathways that enable, inspire and reward high performance. *Give them what they need to grow.*

4.   Reward with **increasing responsibilities** that incentivize the high performers you're building to stick around. As they increase in capacity, *put them in positions where they help others grow.*

The simple reality is that an individual's attitude, values, and skills are not static. How we treat, train, and empower our staff greatly impact how they can ultimately contribute to the organization.

One technician I met was just coming off an incredibly hard patch in life. His previous career aspirations had fizzled out, and he had been sidelined in an unsatisfying job. During his first interview, it was obvious he didn't have a large technology background, but he was articulate and attentive. It was also clear he was motivated to do whatever it took to change his situation.

After follow-up interviews, a few homework assignments, and some phone calls, my team and I agreed. We felt strongly that he had the right attitude and we were reasonably sure he had the aptitude as well. So we hired him for a probationary period.

He was fantastic. A quick learner, he was resolving longstanding issues before he had completed his initial train-up period. We placed him on an aggressive development track and, within his first 18 months, he had achieved two professional IT certifications and had become a trusted member of our core team.

To be clear, nothing here is opposed to the clear wisdom of Schmidt and Rosenberg. Smart hiring is vital. However, when we can't out-bid or out-cool competing job offers for exactly what we want today, we can hire for potential and build what we'll need tomorrow. Most of us don't need savants - we do need smart, engaged, honest, and dedicated staff who care about the organization's success.

This approach works particularly well with Ultralight because of the reduced emphasis on legacy technology. Organizations still need a competent team, but the bulk of the IT workload is no longer in complex local systems management. This frees IT leadership to hire smart people interested in learning rather than current experts with a deep legacy skillset. Hiring is first about attitude and aptitude.

The key is to identify from the pool of the willing those with the aptitude to understand and integrate technology into the organization. Frankly, a quick thinker should be able to grasp foundational management of an Ultralight platform in a few months. But, like a new soldier, it isn't enough to pass through basic training. Continuous development must become a core part of the organization's culture.

Developing an Awesome IT team

Hiring for aptitude only works if that aptitude is aggressively converted into real skill. To do this, every IT team should have a plan to develop their staff with a focus on three core areas:

1. **Technical knowledge** - College courses, professional certifications, structured training, in-office labs, and conference attendance are all appropriate for junior team members. At higher levels, however, the focus should transition from consumption to production. Consider involvement in local and industry communities, best practice research and development, or contributing to industry publications and events.

The litmus test for success here is simple: do upcoming technology trends feel like bright opportunities or treacherous labyrinths? A team dedicated to technical learning should have the confidence to not only face impending change, but embrace and even pioneer it.

2. **Interpersonal skill** - There are worse places to start than a discussion of temperament from the Myers-Briggs or Keirsey perspective, with an emphasis on the contrasts between and need for different perspectives. Emotional intelligence, team dynamics, and conflict resolution fit here.

3. **Leadership competence** - This is too vast to cover in-depth here, but some areas to consider are listed below. Ultimately, personnel management must be oriented around strong IT leaders who can build teams and drive change.

- **Character traits** - make leadership about doing the right thing, and be clear about how this applies in the organization

- **Practical skills** - include management requirements in your organization, task and project management, finance and budgeting training, and other readily quantifiable skills

- **Development pathways** - provide increasing challenges over time that push (but don't burn-out) aspiring leaders

- **Philosophy of leadership** - this is the exciting stuff that everyone reads and writes about, but far fewer people ever actually exercise because they've omitted the previous three elements of leadership competence

Technical skills are important, but they are not more important than the others. Everyone in IT should be willing to work with internal customers. There are few (if any) pure administrators. The IT support team should be constantly interacting with users, and IT leaders should be actively engaging with leaders across your organization.

This means IT staff need interpersonal and leadership skills as well as technical understanding. To develop these skills, leaders must make it a priority.

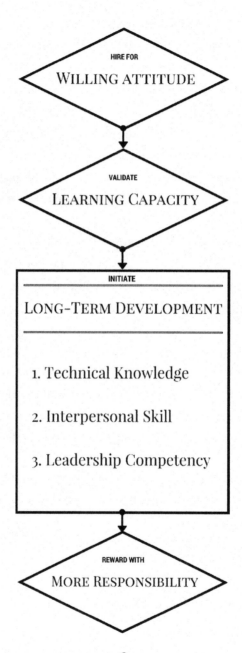

In my most recent shop, we dedicated blocks of time weekly for professional development. This was time away from the desk to focus on targeted objectives including professional certifications, college courses, and independent projects.

For the newest members of the staff, the focus was almost entirely technical. For more experienced staff, the focus transitioned from technical to management and communication skills. Everyone was involved in some level of leadership training with the expectation we'd promote from within. Throughout the various kinds of training, the overarching goal was constant: convert aptitude to skill, and make our team the best it could be.

A culture dedicated to developing internal talent has a number of positive effects. People want to be where they are valued, and investing in them demonstrates in a very tangible way the organization's confidence in their capabilities and worth. And by creating space to let them choose the specific focus of their development, staff advance their personal goals and the organization's goals simultaneously.

These win-win scenarios help keep good people around longer, one of the most critical elements to long-term success. Strong retention allows the IT team to build relationships across the organization, better understand what users need, and develop a deep hands-on knowledge of the environment and systems. It is this knowledge and experience that positions the IT team to provide the greatest possible value.

Real Security

Joe is the security manager of a medieval castle. The essence of a castle's security is, presumably, its walls. So he spends the bulk of his time directing the digging, stacking, and filling of these walls. His challenge is that the castle keeps growing, and he finds it almost impossible to keep up with construction. Some parts of the castle sprawl outside the walls and other sections are barely more than a hump of dirt.

To speed construction, Joe pulls all his available resources. There's no one left to occupy the towers, police the streets, guard the gateways, or conduct counterespionage. But progress on the walls continues faster than ever. Joe is finally making headway when the unthinkable happens - he discovers the treasury has been completely plundered.

He doesn't have any idea who did it, he doesn't even know exactly how long it's been empty. It is a catastrophe.

At this point, Joe's boss begins to understand his challenge: the castle needs even better walls, and Joe needs more resources to keep building. Of course, building bigger walls does nothing to actually deter the clever thief, and Joe's castle keeps getting plundered. And every time it happens, Joe uses the opportunity to argue for greater investment in the walls.

Eventually, there are so many walls, gates, barriers, and blind alleys that the castle interior becomes an impenetrable maze. Only the most experienced citizens dare to wander beyond their immediate vicinity, and communication and transportation are hopelessly gridlocked. There is no single, accurate map of the castle, and every attempt to create one has been foiled by ongoing change.

Still, Joe's castle keeps getting plundered.

This is, more or less, the state of information security today in many organizations. Too many IT teams are still using a *"build bigger walls"* approach to defending their organization, and it just doesn't work. Chris Roland, an information security veteran and CEO of security firm Bastille, notes, "Fortifying walls and leaving the door unlocked is not a strategy."[12]

---

[12]https://www.bastille.io/blogs/will-the-iot-mean-the-end-of-defense-in-depth-cyber-security

Security beyond the walls

An Ultralight security strategy transitions away from the "wall building" paradigm and focuses instead on strengthening three critical areas:

1. **Simple visibility:** know what matters most, in real-time
2. **User empowerment:** make security good for users too
3. **Resilient design:** build systems that are strengthened by shock

The first thing a holistic assessment of our security should reveal is what we've already discovered: we simply can't do everything well. Amazon, Google, and Microsoft can support a much more sophisticated security baseline than we can in our small shops. Let them. Running cloud-based infrastructure lets the *wall-building experts build the walls*, while we focus on the bigger security picture. This is the healthy interdependence that a solid cloud-based platform enables.

With the construction of the walls in the hands of experts who can do it better and more cheaply, we can start to identify where our security time is best spent. Prioritizing effectively requires end-to-end visibility of how users communicate and collaborate. The objective at first isn't to fix problems. It is just to know, *really know*, what is happening to information in the organization.

Once we know what is actually happening, we can start looking for ways to grow resilience in our organization. And the best place to start is with people. It is time to transition from viewing users as security liabilities and start seeing them as security enablers. Focus on training staff and provide them with everything they need to easily get work done securely.

It isn't enough to lock down accounts and engage draconian controls. If we're forcing users to work around our security systems to complete day-to-day tasks, we're digging our own grave. Eventually, we simply won't know where the real risks are. Instead, we must engage with users and find ways to fail-proof their security experience while *enhancing* their sense of control and productivity.

When things do go wrong, we need to resist knee-jerk reactions and look to root causes. By focusing on lasting solutions, we can build more resilient systems and business practices. These can help us understand our environment, respond to the unexpected, adapt quickly to change, and recover from shock stronger than when we started.

The power of visibility

It is tempting to turn a blind eye to what is really going on with information security today. In the IT world, there is a growing body of conflicting opinions written about *Shadow IT*. In short, Shadow IT is an expression for all the technology users have brought from the consumer world into the business world...without asking the IT department first.

As consumer technology capabilities have increased and costs have dropped, IT departments have been unable to keep up. In the past, the *First Platform* was relatively easy to control. Users weren't going to buy their own mainframe even if they did have a deep desire to crunch numbers in their basement. And no one was going to tuck a room-filling mainframe into their bag and walk out the door.

The rise of the PC complicated office security. Protecting local networks and managing business PCs became an industry. Beyond malicious actors, the focus was largely on stopping office users from doing or accessing more than was necessary for their job. Businesses downgraded the rights of most users so they couldn't install programs or change trivial settings. Everything users needed came preinstalled by the administrator, and users worked as if the PC were a fancy mainframe terminal. The good old days were back!

This has all changed. Today, cloud-based business software can often do *for free* what complex legacy software can't do *at all*. Communication and collaboration through Facebook, Slack, Office 365 and countless other offerings are an Internet connection away, and new products appear faster than network administrators can block them.

The *Second Platform* problem was preventing users from doing the wrong thing with business resources. Computer management products from that era could control every last detail of how a PC functioned. Don't want employees putting pictures of their families on the desktop? Fixed! Want to make Internet Explorer crash on every webpage but the corporate homepage? Done! Tired of poorly supervised workers playing Solitaire? Got it covered.

The problem now is fundamentally different. Today, employees aren't trying to do personal stuff with business resources, they're *moving the business* onto their personal devices and cloud services. They're doing this because these new tools offer a genuinely faster, easier, and more reliable way to get things done.

To develop a comprehensive security strategy in this new world, organizations must first actually know where their data is and how staff get work done. With Ultralight, this process is straightforward. Because all user activity is associated with a single digital identity, it is possible to develop a comprehensive picture of what each user is doing, sharing, and accessing.

Today's cloud-based security tools can monitor every file share and third-party application. Cloud-based inventory and authentication tools make it possible to evaluate mobile or traditional hardware in use by everyone associated with the organization. When these tools are combined, organizations can track every user, share, application, and hardware device connecting to business data. They can do it regardless of who owns the device or when the app was released, and they can do it in real-time.

This level of visibility is nearly impossible to achieve apart from a cloud-based platform. The system-centric management views of the PC era are too fragmented to map user behavior holistically. This is one of the reasons why Ultralight can be both *simpler* and *more secure* for small businesses than a legacy-based platform.

Once IT achieves visibility, they can start developing robust policies to protect that data. However, to generate the greatest value from those policies and ensure they maintain visibility requires something more.

IT must invite users into the security paradigm so they fight *for* the organization instead of *against* it. That means making security good for the users too.

Security for the people

I've seen organizations where, attempting to be "user-focused", *security* becomes a bad word. Embracing the idea that security is inherently restrictive, these organizations ignore or sideline it as much as possible. They believe productivity gains from ignoring security will outweigh the risks. *"Besides, who cares enough to hack us anyway?"*

But many losses aren't related to high-profile hacking or malicious activity. Rather, a user accidentally overwrites an important file, or the power flickers and brings down the system right before a critical presentation. Users feel like they are forever walking on thin ice. This insecurity complicates users' lives, creating frustration and reducing productivity. Organizations can't ignore security and be truly user-focused.

By contrast, I have seen some organizations where the relationship between users and the information security manager is, at best, antagonistic. Users are constantly trying to circumvent the organization's security so they can get their job done. Meanwhile, the security manager is struggling to plug the holes users create with all their workarounds. This infighting wastes an enormous amount of time and energy, and the net security posture at the end is typically worse than when it all started.

Both types of organizations - the oblivious and the antagonistic - make the same fundamental error about how users should relate to information security: both believe the relationship between users and security is inherently adversarial.

Ultralight rejects this idea. Great security should make life easier for users, and the more it does so, the more readily users will buy into a healthy security paradigm. Applying a user empowering approach to security is about finding win-win solutions.

Win-win includes things like reliable, transparent, user-accessible backups. Great backups are a simple way to tell users their time is valuable in addition to being foundational to a strong security posture. A simple, consistent form of single sign-on is also a win-win, allowing IT to track users holistically while reducing the complexity of their day-to-day tasks.

Users should never lose data. Users should never lose connectivity. If time or data is lost, IT should make it a critical task to identify why and work to ensure it doesn't happen again. Similarly, when users do violate policies or introduce new risks, the first step should be to assess why they felt the need. Risky activities should trigger a discussion before they trigger a lockdown, allowing IT to learn where they can streamline workflows or reduce friction between users and systems.

By making increased security correlate with increased capability and service, it is much easier to generate user buy-in. Building a reservoir of goodwill gives IT leadership the latitude for those times when staff must make real concessions in the name of security. This increased trust also builds a strong foundation for one of the most critical elements of information security: user training.

User training and education are central to Ultralight. Organizational leaders must understand how the cloud can transform business processes before they'll glean the full value of the technology. The same is true for users, particularly where security is concerned. This includes educating users about the benefits of new technologies, increasing their awareness of cyber security threats, and making them a valued part of ongoing security efforts.

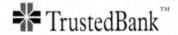 TrustedBank™

Dear valued customer of TrustedBank,

We have recieved notice that you have recently attempted to withdraw the following amount from your checking account while in another country: $135.25.

If this information is not correct, someone unknown may have access to your account. As a safety measure, please visit our website via the link below to verify your personal information:

http://www.trustedbank.com/general/custverifyinfo.asp

Once you have done this, our fraud department will work to resolve this discrepency. We are happy you have chosen us to do business with.

Thank you,
TrustedBank

Member FDIC © 2005 TrustedBank, Inc.

I worked with one astute security manager who collected reports of potential phishing emails. Once a month, he would take an actual phishing attempt and turn it into an instructional bulletin discussing the warning signs for malicious messages. While his humorous emails provided useful tips for users, these messages had a greater value. His emails honored the users who had successfully detected real phishing attack. This recognition helped reinforce the fact that the battle was IT and the staff working together *against the hackers*, not IT working *against the staff.*

Of course, where we had automated ways to eliminate phishing emails, we pursued them. But with his monthly emails, this manager empowered users and increased the organization's resilience. He used actual attacks to educate and encourage the staff, which is both user-centered and the essence of resilient security.

A resilient approach to security

> "There are two kinds of big companies in the United States. There are those who've been hacked by the Chinese and those who don't know they've been hacked by the Chinese."
> ~ FBI Director James Comey, 2014[13]

Big, complex systems designed to stop specific threats are untenable. The threats we face today evolve much faster than we can develop defenses, and what defenses we have are costly to build and sustain. Each new protection requires more resources, more effort, and more complexity.

In The Age of the Unthinkable, Joshua Cooper Ramo proposes an alternative. Rather than trying to build walls against every possible threat (a demonstrably failing strategy), he recommends we broaden our perspective and find ways to replace fragile, specialized systems

---

[13]http://www.businessinsider.com/fbi-director-china-has-hacked-every-big-us-company-2014-10

with flexible, resilient systems. Ultralight draws from this insight to lay out a more realistic approach to IT security based on the resilience concept.

General (Ret.) Stanley McChrystal describes resilience thinking this way:

> "'Resilience thinking' is a burgeoning field that attempts to deal in new ways with the new challenges of complexity. In a resilience paradigm, managers accept the reality that they will inevitably confront unpredicted threats; rather than erecting strong, specialized defenses, they create systems that aim to roll with the punches, or even benefit from them... like immune systems, [they] can benefit from shocks."[14]

Nothing is 100% secure. It is only a matter of time before even the best defenses are breached, before a user makes a critical error, before the one thing that *can't* fail...fails. FBI Director Comey's observation about the Chinese hacking threat speaks to this reality. And if the Chinese are doing it, others are too.

Comey's statement also illuminates the only real differentiation between security teams: awareness. The question isn't whether or not successful attacks have occurred, but whether or not companies know it, and know what was lost, and understand how to respond.

For this reason, the first step toward establishing a resilient security posture must be to attain the visibility described previously. Once the

---

[14]From <u>Team of Teams</u>

IT team has achieved visibility, they can begin to take meaningful actions. How IT implements resilient security will depend heavily on the specific organization, but there are a number of foundational actions that can help regardless.

1. **Know what really matters** - Carefully identify what is most vital to the organization's success. Think holistically about the organization's values and what differentiates it from other organizations. Use this knowledge to map out the highest-value security opportunities in the organization right now. Guide security decisions using the long-view, looking toward big goals and core values. This will make it much easier to weigh the opportunity costs of a security decision.

2. **Contemplate the apocalypse** - With a clear understanding of what really matters, talk about the types of failures that would most hurt the organization. Then, explore how to fail gracefully and recover quickly. Consider not just *prevention* but *response* as well. What can IT do now to reduce the impact of a failure? What policies and processes can be put in place to respond more effectively when a failure occurs? Like regular school fire drills, small preparation efforts up front can drastically reduce loss during an actual emergency.

3. **Enjoy the low-hanging fruit** - There are low effort, high return security opportunities in most environments today. Identify, prioritize and act on these opportunities. Avoid spending large amounts of time or money trying to get an 80% solution up to 90% while there are still key weaknesses sitting untouched. Do staff use

two-step authentication? Do all systems have encrypted disks? Is mobile device management in place? If the answer to any of these questions is "no", the organization likely has some low-hanging fruit. Don't get distracted gilding the castle's parapets before there are working locks on the doors.

4. **Make user success the center of security** - Educate and empower users. Let them be the eyes and ears of the security strategy. Generate buy-in, celebrate user victories, and work proactively with staff when implementing new technologies. Integrate the IT team into different business units to help anticipate needs and concerns. Work with, never against, employees. This is the only way to ensure IT maintains the visibility and authority necessary to actually secure the organization.

5. **Own your data** - The U.S. government has very strict security rules, yet it failed to secure former Secretary of State Hillary Clinton's emails. She was hosting them on her own server, which meant every other security precaution the government took was moot. If the organization doesn't own its data, it doesn't matter what its policies are. Once IT understands how users are already using cloud technologies in the business, gently consolidate around a platform that puts IT in control of all critical data. Ensure cloud products have a reliable export capability for backups or transfer, and actually *do backups*.

6. **Love simplicity** - Place a massive premium on simplicity when integrating new technology. Consider adapting business processes to fit simple, stable, well-integrated technologies rather

than building a custom database or deploying highly specialized software. Don't reinvent the CRM or ERP. The corollary is to understand the features of existing technology *before adding more*. Users don't need seven different chat applications, no matter how cool the emojis are. Prefer simpler, well-integrated solutions, and implement them fully.

7.   **Deploy durable technologies** - Users should never know when a piece of backend hardware fails. Take advantage of technologies that were built from the ground up with resilience in mind. By contrast, if achieving redundancy is expensive, complicated, or impossible, look elsewhere. Finally, take advantage of cloud-based backup solutions for additional failure protection.

The unexpected becomes far less menacing when administrators have visibility, users are empowered, and systems are simple, flexible, and reliable.

"But", someone says, "Isn't the cloud just a giant single point of failure?"

Let's explore that question for a moment.

How to stop worrying and love the cloud

As we've already discussed, the *Third Platform* is here to stay. Rather, it's here to stay until we discover something better, or the grid truly goes black. If the former, *better* will be even more disconcerting to our present way of thinking than the *Third Platform*. If the latter, the survival of our businesses may be the least of our concerns.

If Google, or Amazon, or Microsoft collapsed overnight it wouldn't matter if we had our data stored locally or in the cloud. Our vendors, customers, municipality, public services, and countless others would be catastrophically impacted and our business along with it. In 2015, 45 million academic users depended on Google Apps[15]. If Google Apps suddenly disappeared, the impact on the education system alone would be apocalyptic.

This situation isn't new. The world we live in is highly interdependent, has been for centuries, and is becoming ever more so. Our prosperity is dependent on global food production, regional logistics, the electric grid, sanitation, and so on. The Internet is now part of that puzzle and our dependence on it will continue to grow. It doesn't matter whether we like it or even if it is truly a good thing. It matters that it is so.

So the question isn't whether or not a major provider is going to submarine the business if it suddenly vaporized. The question is how long the business is going to maintain the horse stable, light the office with oil, and refuse indoor plumbing. This may seem like an overstrong statement, but the point deserves emphasis. Timely technological adoption correlates with real competitive advantage. Organizations ignore major technology shifts at their peril.

In 1994, Wired magazine found only one major television network with a website. This observation alone helps explain why calling these legacy networks *major* feels anachronistic. In their defense, fully half

---

[15]https://boostelearning.com/google-apps-for-education-anticipated-to-reach-110-million-users-by-2020/

of the Fortune 500 didn't have an Internet address back then either, and they didn't understand why they should.

When the Wired journalist attempted to explain to a McDonald's representative why the Internet was important, he was rebuffed. Finally, the journalist simply purchased the *mcdonalds.com* domain himself.[16] McDonald's survived despite its slow start (and did, eventually, ransom its domain name with a charitable contribution), but others have not been so fortunate.

Twenty years ago, a student from Stanford concluded an *Impact of the Internet on Business*[17] study by saying, "It is up to each business to decide if the potential benefits [of the Internet] outweigh the potential risks. Hopefully, we'll see you on the Web!" Looking back, it seems laughable. Email has moved past reliable to become our daily bane, our grandparents all have smartphones, and our children download apps before they can repeat the alphabet.

The *Third Platform*, like the Internet on which it is built, is changing how the world interacts. This involves new interdependencies and incredible opportunities. The dependencies will touch our organizations regardless of the platform we build on. The challenge we face today is how to best take advantage of the opportunities.

---

[16]http://www.wired.com/1994/10/mcdonalds/
[17]http://www-cs-students.stanford.edu/~dwhitney/lisa/IS_Final_Proj.html

Part 1: Better Things

Part 2: Understanding Ultralight

Ultralight creates excellence through simplicity. The goal is to reduce complexity for users so they can focus on being amazing at their jobs. For the IT department, it is about doing fewer things better, so the IT team can be awesome at what it actually needs to do. This requires transitioning core capabilities into the cloud, not overlaying cloud tech as a hosted solution alongside legacy infrastructure. The key is to replace or avoid not only the classic technology tools, but the entire *Second Platform* methodology.

Facing the Challenge

The IT environment I walked into was chaotic. A quarter of the users were dependent on a partially configured Active Directory domain. Another third relied on a separate local LDAP directory. Some employees used both directories, and about half the staff were in the wild, sharing resources using email, Dropbox, or other third-party solutions.

Some departments only used Macs. Less fortunate users spent their days slogging away on tired netbooks running Windows Vista Starter. Each department had its own way to purchase computers, manage calendars, and coordinate projects. More than half of the staff forwarded organizational emails to personal accounts, and worked out of their personal inbox.

For me and my team of two, it was clear this was unsustainable. It was also clear we couldn't fix it simply by patching together the existing systems. We needed a new approach. We wanted a way to conquer the scope problem and create an awesome IT department, even though we were a very small, very young shop.

When we first went looking for principles to direct our modernization, we found countless suggestions. Most conflicted with one another, introduced complexity we couldn't possibly manage, or recommended products or services we couldn't afford. Amid all the options, we struggled to find a coherent methodology to guide our decision making. Everyone had something to sell, but no one could offer a clear picture of how to bring everything together on a budget with a limited staff.

Ultralight is the set of principles we wish we'd had from the start, a methodology we honed as we worked through the challenges of modernizing our organization. It is a way to support technology in an organization that has better things to do than think about technology, yet still needs awesome IT support to function well. The remainder of this section digs into the four core Ultralight principles and concludes with some hard-learned change management observations.

Excellence-Focused

An obligatory definition

If excellence is *the expression of mastery*, IT professionals deploying Ultralight must achieve mastery *of the organization's relationship with technology.* Understanding this relationship is key to providing amazing support, integrating the best solutions, and empowering staff to achieve success.

To define excellence is one thing; to measure it is another. For our purposes, the simplest measure of IT's level of excellence is *the degree to which IT is trusted within the organization.*

When IT has mastery of not just the tech tools but also of how those tools help staff achieve the organization's goals, IT is in a position to build trust. Of course, to be trusted as a technology professional, we need to be able to recommend, deploy, and maintain reliable systems that meet the organization's needs. But it only starts there.

I'm kicking our ever-present dead horse here: Ultralight is about more than technology. It is about empowering the organization to succeed, and understanding how simplifying and streamlining technology enables this success.

Solve business problems

Nowhere is IT's expertise more vital than the crossing between business needs and technology solutions. The more effective IT is at identifying and solving the rubber-meets-the-road issues their peers are facing, the more valuable IT's technology decisions will be.

While a key part of solving business problems is interpersonal art, at least some part is science and can be aided by repeatable processes. In lieu of a more sophisticated method, the following five questions provide a foundation for digging into business problems and finding solutions:

1. What hurts?
2. What is the root communication challenge?
3. What part of the solution is technological?
4. What does an Ultralight solution look like?
5. How do I implement it as painlessly as possible?

1. What hurts?

The first step is assessing what is working well, what isn't, and what could benefit from new technology. Where are things more difficult than they need to be? Where do users get frustrated? What shadow IT tools are leaders leaking into the organization? What capabilities are on the horizon that could streamline workflows or make users' lives easier?

Build a running list of opportunities, prioritize them, and start working through them.

2. What is the root communication challenge?

Step two is digging down to the root of the problem. Before recommending a technology solution, be sure to understand the heart of the communication challenge. Take time to discuss what fellow leaders want to achieve, what business tasks users are trying to streamline, or how a new technology will impact the organization long-term.

3. What part of the solution is technological?

Very few problems have strictly technological solutions, because most problems involve people. Tech can't fix management ambiguities, poor controls, or user ignorance. The best solutions must address the human side of the equation as well.

At one organization, we had many young staff members with limited professional experience. Users often came to us asking for new technology tools to manage relatively simple tasks. As we dug into what they were really asking, we discovered what they needed were basic business skills, not more technology.

Before they could get any real value from our core platform, we needed to show them foundational time and task management, how to use a calendar, and how to manage personal tasks. To address this, we made skills development part of the initial IT onboarding process, and offered ongoing training.

Had we just done what they asked, we would have obscured - not solved - the root problem. Their issue wasn't strictly technological, but we needed to address it if we wanted to provide awesome IT support to the organization.

4. What does an Ultralight solution look like?

Let's start with what an Ultralight solution *isn't*. It's probably not an augmented reality device. Ultralight depends on new technologies, but it is not about chasing *new* for its own sake. To stay out in front of users, IT must actively explore the latest technologies. But don't confuse educational activities with implementation activities. A portion of IT's time should be dedicated to research and testing, but this study should never short-circuit good decision-making when it's time to solve a real business challenge.

Conversely, there are likely many legacy tools that can address the need but at the cost of added complexity, greater management overhead, and poor user integration. Go back to the core principles. Find a cloud-based product that integrates seamlessly with the core platform, is easy to manage, and provides a great user experience. Ensure the solution is:

Excellence-Focused: To avoid managing redundant systems, only deploy technologies that bring substantial new capabilities. Often, a minor process change or a little education can allow an existing product to solve a new challenge. A complementary strategy is to continually educate staff on what the existing technologies can do.

User-Centered: Solutions must integrate with users' digital identity, and represent the best possible combination of ease-of-use and manageability. Pay attention to the user experience, testing beyond raw feature-set to the way it fits into users' daily workflows.

Cloud-Based: Focus on products that require zero administrative management beyond the application layer, and make sure they integrate with the core platform. If it requires onsite servers, it probably isn't Ultralight. Look for best practices and reference the experience of others. Attend professional conferences where vendors present the latest tools for the organization's core platform. Get connected to the broader community, building awareness of the platform's ecosystem.

Hardware-Minimizing: When hardware is necessary, focus on products that integrate easily with other platforms and tools. Look for systems that favor standards-based integrations, API access, and robust import/export functionality. Equipment oriented around open-source technology isn't a silver bullet, but proprietary hardware that shoehorns IT into closed software is perilous (no matter how great the feature set).

5. How do I implement as painlessly as possible?

Invest time in a deliberate change management process, no matter how urgent the need (and no matter how basic the change management). Have a plan to validate a solution, educate users, deploy in stages, and document and refine the solution. Shooting from the hip is a great way to accidentally kill someone. To build trust, be willing to diligently work through change with leaders and users.

Two kinds of business partners you meet in the cloud

Ultralight starts with the concession we can't do it all alone. Instead, we need a team of trusted partners around us. Building this team is critical to success with Ultralight, from the core cloud provider to the local ISP. To understand how to identify strong partners, we first have to understand the two fundamentally different types of cloud solutions sold today.

Cloud is an ambiguous marketing term, and it seems like everyone is selling a web-enabled, Internet-accessible version of their product. But there is a world of difference between products and services that were *built from the ground up* as Third Platform tools (which I'll refer to as *cloud-born*), and those that have been *retrofitted* to work in the cloud (or *cloud-enabled*).

For our purposes, cloud-born is typically good, and cloud-enabled is typically not. Everything else being equal, cloud-born services provide more for less.[18] Modern datacenter operating systems, container-based application management, and commoditized hardware provide remarkable efficiency, scale, and reliability. As these technologies mature, vendors have tremendous market pressure to pass increased savings and capabilities down the line.

Developing, scaling, and integrating cloud-born solutions is trivial compared to the requirements of the local-network server applications of old. Rapid-growth startups like Snapchat, Reddit, Spotify, Pinterest and many others have leveraged cloud platforms from Google or Amazon to provide robust, reliable infrastructure with minimal overhead and streamlined integration.[19] Their business models depend on this power and simplicity.

---

[18]Cloud-born services may also offer substantially greater security by employing multi-instance (each client in a distinct environment) rather than multi-tenant (all clients in one massive database) architecture. This is a more complex topic than I can do justice to here, but the discussion reinforces the importance of understanding the differences between - and relative merits of - different cloud architectures.

[19]http://www.businessinsider.com/snapchat-is-built-on-googles-cloud-2014-1

By contrast, cloud-enabled products and services must try to hide their legacy complexity, typically by abstracting it away with some form of virtualization. But virtualization is just a bandaid. Application virtualization does indeed let IT push legacy products across the Internet almost as if they were a true web service. But the legacy requirements of cloud-enabled products typically bleed through in the form of higher cost, greater complexity, and reduced interoperability.

Not every solution an organization needs can come from a *cloud-born* provider today. Decades of legacy development have led to some amazing products that have yet to be eclipsed by Third Platform solutions. And poor code is poor code, whether it is in the cloud or on a physical machine; that a developer is using Google Compute Engine doesn't tell us anything about the quality of the product itself. Finally, many business capabilities simply don't exist (or lack key functionality) in the cloud-born space.

Still, deploying Ultralight is biased toward cloud-born. The power and flexibility of today's datacenter operating systems represent a fundamental shift in what's possible. As time goes on, it will become ever easier to find cloud-born solutions that allow us to increase capabilities, minimize costs, and greatly reduce complexity for organizations.

Build a strong team of excellence-focused partners

To succeed, most organizations will need a team of trusted partners to provide insight, expertise, and support. With this in mind, I've included a series of observations to inspire discussion. Some of these observations may be controversial, but I hope they are useful just the same when exploring what matters most to your organization.

The technologies that enable Ultralight operations are often very new. Many of the companies developing and deploying the best tools for Ultralight are startups, industry disrupters, or rogue divisions of old-guard businesses. As such, they may not be as organizationally stable or technologically mature as classic providers. This creates a challenge: how do we balance the need for stability against the benefits of working with innovators?

The good news is that the two core platforms enabling Ultralight, Microsoft's Office 365 and Google Apps for Work, aren't going anywhere. The add-ons, integrations and additional capabilities an organization needs, however, will come from a range of other vendors. Choosing them wisely is vital to smooth operations. When assessing these vendors, consider the following:

Read the contracts

Contracts are critical for building healthy partnerships, but only if they are balanced. Data ownership, service level agreements, and termination charges should be areas of special attention. How service issues and disputes are resolved, and determination of who is legally responsible for breaches or failures should be clearly understood.

A more simplistic form of this rule is avoiding companies that pursue excessively long contracts. I once had the misfortune of finding I'd inherited a technology contract that was seven years long, with a company whose attitude toward customers could best be described as contemptuous. The contract was worded in such a way that the customer was a hopeless pawn forced to accept all the risk with little recourse to address problems.

Ultimately, contracts should be the fences that make good neighbors - not chains that shackle IT budgets to the proverbial oars. Most cloud service providers offer a discount for year-to-year pricing, and this can offer stability and value. In some instances, a two or even three year agreement may be appropriate, but these should be very carefully considered. Make sure contract details and timelines fit the goals and trajectory of the organization.

Look for signs of health

Marketing copy, technical specs, and online reviews can all be useful, but they aren't the whole equation. When looking for strong business partners, the *people* matter as much as the brand. This is true from the executive leadership all the way to the sales or service person who actually answers the questions and solves the problems. Consider carefully the culture and leadership of the organization.

The best local service organizations I work with share a common trait: unusually high employee tenure. Even the service engineers have decades with the companies, and the quality of service is typically outstanding. Whatever else is true, the leadership has created a culture that inspires loyalty, and this has translated into a highly experienced team capable of amazing service.

In emerging fields where even the trailblazing organizations are only a few years old, no employee will have decades of tenure. But it is still possible to get a sense for the culture, whether or not the startup team has worked together before, and other signs of health (or dysfunction) on the staff.

Get an excellent core, than keep it simple

There is always going to be a tension between excellence and simplicity. Purchasing best-of-breed for *everything* means very few products will have the same vendor. This isn't likely to be particularly scalable or highly interoperable.

The compromise is to identify the core elements (the vendors, platforms, or partners) that matter most to achieve excellence, and then to build around these. Suppose an organization that depends heavily on WiFi has already chosen Meraki or Aerohive for cloud management of wireless access points. Now they want to add cloud management for switches as well. If the existing platform's switch solution is good enough, it would be a mistake to deploy a completely new cloud-managed platform for switches alongside the access points. Let key components be excellent, and then keep it simple.

Prefer simpler, cloud-born providers

The previous section covered this in detail, but I'll reiterate it here. Look for cloud-born partners, businesses that are invested in the same operational model we are. The good news is that as time goes on, there will be ever more quality options available. And, if there is any ambiguity, look for simplicity, particularly in the areas of management, scalability, and third-party integration.

A managed service too far

We've previously discussed the need to outsource in a healthy way as much as possible below the application layer. But Ultralight does not outsource everything. Eliminating minutia is essential, but it is possible to go wrong in the other direction and outsource the things onsite IT staff alone can do with excellence.

This is the temptation of relying too heavily on a Managed Service Provider (MSP) or similar outsourcing partner. An MSP is a company that manages IT infrastructure for other organizations. MSPs typically offer subscription services for proactive management. They may also provide break-fix coverage, consulting, hosted products, and other services.

Superficially, Ultralight and an MSP have a lot in common. Both attempt to outsource whatever isn't essential, allowing the business to focus on what matters. But there are critical differences. While MSPs may be able to take a limited role in Ultralight, they can also undermine the value and quality Ultralight is designed to achieve. There are multiple reasons for this.

Ultralight builds value through simplicity

MSPs make more money by adding complexity. A quality MSP can do an admirable job maintaining all the systems that Ultralight eliminates from an environment. They'll do it with additional charges, and costs grow tremendously as the organization grows. Their incentive is to add complexity to the environment, not reduce it.

Ultralight builds on the cloud to solve the scope problem

MSPs have traditionally addressed the scope problem by maintaining a pool of experts and making them available as needed to support customer systems. This approach misses the point. You don't need to timeshare experts to run complex infrastructure because Ultralight eliminates your exposure to that infrastructure entirely. Ultralight is about finding solutions that reduce the organization's need for a cadre of experts.

Ultralight empowers leaders and staff to be awesome

MSPs may outsource decisions and relationships the IT department must control to achieve excellence. Putting an MSP between IT and the users, or between IT and the core platform, reduces insight to critical problems and emerging issues. This exacerbates the challenge of finding the best remedies and can make the business beholden to their (conveniently priced) solutions.

Ultralight frees IT to focus on the user experience as well as finding and integrating the best possible technology solutions. More generally, Ultralight allows an organization to take ownership of IT in a way that wasn't possible when many MSPs came into being. Cloud services provide an economy of scale far beyond what a classic MSP can provide, with greater control and fewer strings attached. As time goes on, MSPs will certainly integrate ever more cloud tech into their offerings, but many of the base tensions will remain.

Having said all this, I'd like to add a caveat. There are a growing number of partner organizations created specifically to enable cloud-based IT, and these organizations can bring tremendous value. This is particularly true for larger, more complex organizations attempting to migrate legacy platforms to the cloud. In many instances, a quality partner can considerably improve an organization's overall satisfaction with a cloud deployment.[20]

The point here isn't that partners, including MSPs, can't provide value. Rather, the key is to understand how they fit into the Ultralight framework. To achieve simplicity, there must be a constant pressure to reduce - not add - extraneous dependencies. To achieve excellence, IT must be fully integrated into the business decision-making, not glued on after the fact. And to provide great service, IT personnel must be available and accountable to the people they serve.

Provide the highest quality in-house tech

All core communication and collaboration should be provided through the cloud, from email and calendar to telephony and file management. Some things, however, will still be managed internally. This includes the network, the service desk, onsite hardware that can't be eliminated, and the ever growing collection of gadgets, sensors, plugins, and tools collectively referred to as the Internet of Things (IoT).

Use the time and resources saved with Ultralight to do these things really, really well. The following chapters dig into this concept in more detail, but the key is to measure value. Ultralight can help save a considerable amount of money, but the goal isn't cost savings alone. The goal is value generation. So don't give all the savings back. Instead, reinvest it in critical infrastructure, in enhancing the user'

---

[20]https://www.bettercloud.com/monitor/state-of-cloud-it-2016/

experience, and in developing IT staff to make them the best they can be.

User-Centered

A schoolhouse, from hire to exit

All business tech exists, presumably, to enable people to do things faster, or more easily, or more effectively. But each piece of technology, as a tool, is made valuable only through the skill of those wielding it.

IT has historically been focused on the tools themselves. The reason is straightforward: systems management demands the bulk of IT's time. Too often, this creates a gap between what an organization's technology *can* do and what users actually *know how* to do with it. Ultralight turns this around, creating space for IT to train and educate staff. This can greatly increase both user satisfaction and the value of deployed technologies.

The core of the user-centered approach is a transition from focusing on systems to focusing on people. To accomplish this transition, IT must become a high-quality schoolhouse capable of developing internal IT talent, the broader user base, and fellow business leaders. This transition deliberately reallocates time from legacy IT activities and reinvests it in development efforts.

How a schoolhouse functions will vary from organization to organization. A user base composed of an unchanging roster of 30-

year veterans will need a different teaching approach than a younger, more volatile workforce. In either case, continual skills development, best practice instruction, and business process improvement should be the standard.

Skills Development

One organization I worked with had a tremendously powerful collaboration platform available to every staff member. But proactive training was non-existent, and users had no idea how to leverage the tools. Sticky notes and gratuitous printouts were the norm despite having robust intranet and integrated communication tools accessible from every computer. The organization never leveraged more than a fraction of the power they were doomed to support and maintain.

Skills development helps avoid this kind of waste. It isn't realistic to believe a pre-deployment crash course is going to empower staff to truly take advantage of a new tool. Skills development must be an ongoing process that certifies users at various levels of competence, encourages staff to take advantage of powerful features, and continually assesses how technology is used and can be improved.

To be clear, this is not an invitation to force everyone into boring quarterly briefings. To the contrary, engagement and genuine buy-in are as critical as the content itself. Only when the two are combined will users embrace the training and get real value from it. It is the responsibility of IT to communicate the value and relevance of training, and then ensure the training is engaging and empowering.

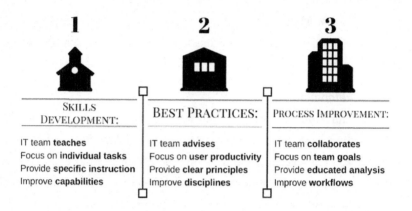

1 Skills Development:	**2** Best Practices:	**3** Process Improvement:
IT team **teaches** Focus on **individual tasks** Provide **specific instruction** Improve **capabilities**	IT team **advises** Focus on **user productivity** Provide **clear principles** Improve **disciplines**	IT team **collaborates** Focus on **team goals** Provide **educated analysis** Improve **workflows**

Best Practice Instruction

It is great to know what all the buttons do in the Calendar or Email App, or how to navigate an application. But it takes something more - a process, a discipline, or a workflow - to turn all the technology tools we use into a coherent system that makes work more manageable. IT can generate tremendous value by bridging the divide between what technology *can do* and what we *ought to do* to be productive.

A user's email inbox often serves as their de-facto task list, a function it was never designed to perform. Likewise, it typically isn't a good sign when an email inbox has 800 unread emails. Yet both are often the case, and the reasons for this are bigger than the specific nuances of email as a tool. The problem isn't that users get too many emails, it is that users don't know how to effectively process and prioritize information. The issue is bigger than technology. To empower these staff members, they need to be taught how to live out a discipline.

For years, my team and I have taught Merlin Mann's *Inbox Zero*[21] concept. It provides a philosophy for thinking about email beyond the computer, for assessing what each email represents and dealing with it rapidly. We've found it to be a very useful way to introduce concepts of ownership and intentionality to knowledge workers, and it segways naturally into more robust personal management systems like David Allen's *Getting Things Done*.

Task management is one of many potential training opportunities. Wherever users are engaging with technology, IT should speak not only to operational requirements, but to the processes, disciplines, and workflows that generate the greatest value.

Finally, by teaching disciplines that transcend specific technologies, schoolhouses empower their staff to succeed even as technologies change. Using our example of task management, the disciplines of intentionality and prioritization bring value whether users rely primarily on pen-and-paper, their email inbox, or a messaging tool like Slack. And those disciplines will continue to provide value whenever the next technology rolls around, creating enormous long-term benefit for the individual and the organization.

Business Process Improvement

The IT schoolhouse exists to empower users, to help fully engage the people side of the technology value equation. While the best practice training just described is focused on individual users, business process improvement expands the view to look at teams, departments, and organization-wide technology use.

---

[21]http://www.43folders.com/izero

As schoolhouse goals become more complex, IT's role must transition from instructional to collaborative. *Skills development*, being relatively straightforward, puts IT in the role of classic instructor. With *best practices training*, IT shifts to an advisor role, helping staff explore and develop personal disciplines. Finally, *business process improvement* focuses IT on research and collaboration. IT transitions from teaching and advising to working directly alongside other organizational decision-makers. This is the post-graduate level of IT support.

Skills required at this level include:

1 **Patience and humility** - Process improvement requires a willingness to ask open questions, receive honest answers, and communicate results clearly and professionally. There is no place for the arrogant expert here. Business leaders must know that you're here to listen and learn, that you don't think you already have the answers, and that you can appreciate their own perspective and expertise.

2 **Knowledge of industry-leading best practices** - Study industry leaders, identify trends, and look for approaches that have weathered challenging integrations. This knowledge will prevent you from reinventing the wheel, freeing you to focus instead on what is uniquely challenging in your organization.

3 **Project Management** - Process improvement will likely require some form of project management. There are numerous methods

available to bring structure and clarity to projects, and IT leaders should be prepared to work within whichever method the organization prefers. If the organization doesn't yet have a structured project management method, IT should be prepared to gently introduce one.

Process improvement is a vast field, and far beyond the scope of this book. But it is too critical to be ignored or relegated to the "*I'll get to it when I get to it*" bucket, a home all too common when IT teams are in survival mode. Ultralight creates space for IT to refocus on the things that matter most, and deliberate process improvement is vital.

Operating at this level is challenging. Done right, however, it is one of the most rewarding places for IT to be.

Run the best service desk

A service desk is similar to a helpdesk, only better. The term "service desk" comes from the Information Technology Infrastructure Library (ITIL), a collection of technology-related best practices that have been refined over the last 30 years into a powerful framework for managing a variety of business functions, including IT.

The transition from "help" to "service" is about shifting from reactive to proactive operations. In ITIL, the service desk acts first as a single point of contact for technology issues, ensuring IT has a clear, comprehensive picture of what is working and what isn't. This knowledge allows the service desk to not just fix immediate issues, but engage in comprehensive problem management. Problem management is about root cause analysis, going past the immediate issue to discover how to prevent future instances of the problem.

The service desk is the most critical user-facing component of the IT department. The experience users have at the service desk has a tremendous impact on their level of confidence in the entire IT team. Even if systems generally run well, poor support experiences can catastrophically alter a user's view of IT (incidentally, this principle also explains why I'm no longer with a certain wireless carrier). Conversely, if the organization has a long road to travel before best practices are widely implemented, great experiences at the service desk can help generate the staff support and buy-in vital to successful change initiatives.

Many organizations struggle to run an awesome service desk. Too often, the service desk is run on life-support. The life-support approach insists on viewing the service desk exclusively as a cost center, believing "the less the organization spends, the less they waste". This forces the service desk team to operate in survival mode, with burned-out technicians putting out fires and gaming trouble tickets.

Rather, the service desk should be a *value generator* for the organization. Users with great IT support spend less time waiting for broken stuff to be fixed, which means they spend more time doing their jobs. These productivity gains have *measurable* financial benefits for the organization. Learning to document and communicate this value within the organization can help transform the service desk into a trusted asset that produces documented returns. IT departments that refuse to identify this value are throwing away a strong argument for investing in a great service desk team.

But not every organization takes the life-support approach. Others instead view the helpdesk as a pariah, and attempt to outsource as much of it as possible. This typically means relying on a managed service provider (MSP). With Ultralight, however, the service desk is too important to outsource, and there are a few reasons for this:

1. **The service desk defines how the organization sees IT**. Both shoestringing and outsourcing the service desk ignore a critical reality: it is the one place where the rest of the organization regularly interfaces with IT. The experience they have with the service desk may decide how they view everything else IT does. The service desk is where the IT team proves (or doesn't) that it really cares about users.

2. **The service desk is a valuable proving ground for new tech hires**. The best way to ensure you have the leadership and expertise you need is to develop it yourself. The service desk provides a place to bring new IT staff onboard, introduce them to the environment, and test their ability to perform. This implies, of course, that IT leadership provides service desk staff avenues for development and growth.

3. **The service desk is where IT learns what is and isn't working**. This includes how the business is actually using technology, and what training and support users need. It is critical for building the trust IT needs to successfully roll out new technology or drive change.

A strong service desk plays an important role in sustaining a user-centered IT team. It is typically the first exposure new employees have to the IT department, and it dominates how most employees will view the quality of organizational IT. The service desk also provides a pipeline for inducting fresh IT staff into the organization. Finally, feedback and lessons learned on the service desk provide essential information for technology decision making across the organization.

Quantify user satisfaction

Resources like ITIL provide a wide array of best practices for successful IT operations. Starting from zero with a small team, however, can be a difficult place to begin. It takes time to understand and incorporate best practices, and the bootstrapping process will likely expose many challenges.

With that said, if IT can only make one change today, it should be this: *start measuring user satisfaction quantitatively.*

The pursuit of greater customer satisfaction will require IT to implement a variety of improvements, but the first step is knowing where things stand today. This is what getting baseline measurements helps accomplish.

I recommend finding an automated way to measure satisfaction. Many incident tracking applications include some form of customer satisfaction reporting, and this should be enabled and monitored. As always, start simple. Any data is better than no data, and a simple *yes* or *no* question is perfectly sufficient to begin.

Negative responses should be actioned immediately to find out where things went wrong and what IT can improve. Don't fall into the trap of blame shuffling. The goal isn't to assess blame, but to prevent failures from happening again. There is *always* something IT can do to make things better.

If systems have been the focus at the expense of users, quantitative satisfaction measurement can help provide accountability while sending a clear message about IT's shift to user-focused operations. Speaking anecdotally, I find (no matter what I say about my intrinsic work ethic) the knowledge that users will measure my performance challenges me to think twice about how I interact with them.

Stay out in front

> "The issue we have... is that for a long time we've introduced IT (a historically structured and binary domain) to make us more productive and there's no question that this has yielded results. I'd argue though to be competitive this is no longer enough. Computers are getting much better at understanding us now as they are more powerful and can learn and adapt. Perhaps then we need to consider putting more emphasis on how IT can help us liberate and personalise our experience rather than just standardise and automate."
> ~ Anthony Stevens, CIO and Entrepreneur[22]

To be user-centered, IT must know what users need today - but that isn't enough. IT must also be able to anticipate and speak to what

[22]https://www.linkedin.com/pulse/people-trump-process-anthony-stevens

they'll want tomorrow. As Anthony Stevens notes, the era where technology is exclusively about process automation is coming to a close. A user-focused IT shop will need to understand the full spectrum of opportunities that emerging technologies create.

Getting and staying out in front is a discipline, and requires a deliberate investment of time and energy.

1. **Achieve understanding:** *study emerging technologies and technology trends* - this includes staying abreast of new capabilities, use cases, implementation approaches, and industry pioneers.

2. **Create options:** *conduct ongoing experimentation and testing* - IT should have a lab environment that allows the team to regularly experiment with emerging technologies. The purpose of a lab is to grow understanding and create options, which means it is more than just a pre-deployment environment. It is a place where IT can build a better understanding of what is possible.

3. **Identify opportunities:** *engage peer leaders* - IT leaders should actively engage with peer leaders to better understand existing processes and future goals. A clear understanding of what is possible and what the organization needs puts IT in a great position to help streamline - or transform - business processes.

Cloud-Based

One login to rule them all

The Second Platform requires users to manage many sets of credentials: local device profiles, encryption keys, countless web applications, secondary verification codes, mobile pins, and on it goes. Active Directory and LDAP allow some level of consolidation, but extending these tools to personal devices, mobile platforms, and cloud applications typically involves ever greater levels of cost and complexity.

With Ultralight, the goal is to tie every authentication action to a single digital identity. The core of this identity should be the Google or Microsoft user account, allowing users to easily access every service they need with their primary organizational login. From system logins to web applications and sharing permissions, a single digital identity makes it easy for users to securely access services and collaborate with other users.

It also provides a much simplified mechanism for administrators to manage user access to corporate data. When a user account is disabled, access is denied to *every* system or service that user employed. And because user access, sharing, and permissions are tied through a single mechanism, it becomes possible to analyze user behavior holistically across systems.

For more complex environments, a number of identity-as-a-service providers make it possible to extend robust security controls through

Google Apps or Microsoft 365. OneLogin, AirWatch, JumpCloud, and others provide a variety of powerful identity management and directory service capabilities, and it is all linked to and managed through the user's single digital identity.

Available anywhere, on any device, all the time

Make the Internet the organization's network, allowing users to get work done wherever they go, on whatever device they have. Users should only need two things to get work done: *valid authentication* and an *Internet-connected device*. This is the incredible simplicity enabled by the cloud, and it drastically reduces complexity for both users and administrators.

To be clear, this is a cloud-based approach to universal connectivity. The legacy approach to achieve ubiquitous access has been through the use of VPNs and - for the truly daring - application virtualization. Both are cumbersome to deploy, use, support, upgrade, and replace. And because they are workarounds for problems that don't exist with purely cloud-based operations, Ultralight makes them unnecessary.

A VPN allows users to remotely connect to the local network to access locally hosted services - services which Ultralight eliminates. When all core user-facing services are cloud-based, there is no need for users to fight with a VPN. This keeps network and endpoint configurations simple.

Where VPNs bring the remote user to onsite applications, application virtualization attempts to bring onsite applications to the remote user. But it is no less cumbersome and complex. Administrators are still responsible for managing and securing the entire technology stack, precisely what Ultralight is designed to prevent. Again, replacing traditional applications with cloud-born services should makes this unnecessary.

Both VPNs and application virtualization have helped bridge the gap between the Second and Third Platform, but both are build on PC-era ideas. True cloud-born services should be easier, safer, and more economical to deploy, eliminating the need for application virtualization.

Master the core cloud platform

To get the most from cloud-based infrastructure, organizations must master the core platform. The time saved no longer managing hardware should be reinvested here, where a deep understanding of capabilities, limitations, third-party integrations, and customizations are critical.

Two platforms today are robust enough to build a comprehensive Ultralight organization around: Microsoft 365 and Google Apps for Work. Both platforms have sufficient core strength and third-party support for cloud-based operations. Each have advantages and disadvantages as well, and the best deployments will play to strengths while mitigating weaknesses.

Organizations that are serious about getting the most value from their core platform should consider the following:

1. **Core Platform Partner** - A number of organizations have arisen in the past five years specializing in cloud-based operations using Microsoft and Google products. A good partner will be able to provide emerging best practice guidance, third-party integration recommendations, deployment and migration assistance, and support for technical issues.

2. **Certifications and Training** - Ongoing administrator training ensures an organization's staff knows what right looks like and how to make it happen. Once an organization is committed to a core platform, baseline certifications are a must for the technical team. Ongoing training can take a number of forms, including formal courses, conference attendance, or web-based training.

3. **Community Blogs and Forums** - Cloud technologies are evolving rapidly, and their uses are as diverse as the organizations that employ them. Look for technical communities focused on similar organizations to see how they are taking advantage of cloud technologies. Connect to vendor and partner blogs, core platform forums, and other centers for discussion and collaboration.

There is a real danger here. Organizations hoping to solve their problems with "better technology" without fully understanding the nature, function, and limitations of that technology will be doomed to frustration and disappointment. The cloud offers tremendous power, simplicity, and security, but only when organizations commit to understanding these capabilities.

Move up the stack

Very few of us ever get to deploy technology in a completely green field - there is always something in place already, even if it is just the startup leadership team's favorite set of tools. This means transitioning to the Third Platform is more about embracing an ongoing process than reaching a static destination.

In practical terms, IT must lay out a roadmap from legacy to Ultralight operations. The basic goal should be to eliminate as much of the technology stack as possible below the application layer. Virtual Machines are better than physical machines, but scalable containers are better than a VM cluster.

To prioritize this roadmap, consider the following:

1 **Pursue highest return first** - Nearly everything can be pushed to the cloud, but not everything has the same value to the organization. Work back from broad user capabilities to unique administrative processes, with an emphasis on first bringing the most benefit to the most users.

2 **Push for 100% user independence** - There may be onsite systems required for back-end functions, but all user-facing applications - capabilities that users rely on for day-to-day operations - should be cloud-based. The litmus test: if it can cause an outage users will notice, it should be a high priority for replacement with a robust cloud-based solution.

3 **Don't take unnecessary half-steps** - Moving legacy systems to a hosted environment is not the same as transitioning to a cloud-based solution. Virtualizing a traditional server is not the same as shifting onto a true container-oriented datacenter OS. Don't waste time taking half-steps that still leave the real opportunities unaddressed. If there is a truly Ultralight solution to a problem, don't waste time and money doing less.

4 **Iterate up as required** - Having warned about half-steps, the reality is that not every system will lend itself to instant movement to the cloud. One environment required us to iterate our voice system first from PRI to SIP, and then from SIP to fully cloud-based voice. This process allowed us to work out bandwidth concerns, clarify exactly what we were going to need for cloud-based operations, and save a considerable amount of money along the way. Look for ways to get closer to Ultralight, and watch out for seemingly exciting technologies that actually take the organization backwards.

5 **Enclave legacy systems** - Sometimes it is not possible to leave a legacy system behind. Cloud-based printing, for instance, is still notoriously unreliable without a local Windows-based server. Complex call centers, onsite backups for large production systems, and other business needs may require onsite systems as well. In these cases, work to enclave these deployments and minimize their technical requirements. The key is to continually reduce complexity, resisting interesting but unnecessary features that create new dependencies.

Provide incredible Internet connectivity

Awesome Internet accessibility and reliability are key to a happy Ultralight environment. If an organization has physical offices, Internet connectivity at those locations should be the best users have ever experienced. This concept should inform infrastructure budgeting and direct how to deploy the network. To do this well:

1   **Have a great firewall:** Don't let the firewall be the network's bottleneck (that is the ISP's role). Competition has driven down prices, and high-bandwidth, high-quality firewalls are more attainable than ever. A good firewall will also provide analytics tools to show how employees use the Internet. This will help identify what risks they are most vulnerable to, and fits well into the resilient security model discussed previously.

2   **Make Internet service fast and stable:** Use more than one Internet service provider, and configure the network such that only a regional catastrophe will cause an Internet outage at the organization's offices. This is less about business continuity than it is about daily productivity and user satisfaction, but it has disaster recovery benefits as well.

3   **Make WiFi spectacular:** Next to the firewall or core router, wireless access points will likely be the most crucial network component. The real-world quality of wireless access points are wildly divergent brand-by-brand and line-by-line. Spend the extra time to find the best solution for the organization's environment, and don't believe all the hype. Test before committing. Today, many wireless networks can be managed through the cloud, providing

comprehensive control with no additional onsite hardware. If possible, take advantage of these capabilities.

While the service desk has the greatest active impact on how users view IT, Internet stability can have a powerful passive impact. Rock solid Internet is like owning a reliable car. We don't think about it every day, but high reliability has a big impact on how we judge the total ownership experience. Make Internet connectivity work so well, users forget it's amazing until they're on someone *else's* network.

Understand business continuity in the cloud

While in a moving vehicle, small children are safer in a car seat than they would be sitting on their parent's lap. As a parent, this reality is obvious to my intellect but contrary to my emotions. My child feels safer in my arms.

Our emotional desire to physically "wrap our arms around" the things we want to protect is both very strong and often misleading. To physically reach out and touch the Linux server hosting my website feels like security to me. I feel in control. But if I haven't had time to harden the install, regularly patch the server, monitor the logs, maintain and test backups, analyze network behavior, and ensure it is protected from physical and cyber-attacks, I'm indulging an illusion. The premium we often place on physical proximity is an extension of the car seat fallacy. To achieve higher security, we must do what is less comfortable but more logical.

When we do what is less comfortable, remarkable things become possible.

1   **Business operations are location independent** - When Hurricane Sandy hit New York City in 2012, it cut electrical power throughout the region, disrupted local carriers, and disabled multiple datacenters in the Manhattan area.[23] The only protection from some failures is real geographic separation. Cloud-based platforms can provide this natively, ensuring business operations continue smoothly despite local disasters and other unforeseen failures. And independence from the local LAN ensures that employees can get work done at a nearby Starbucks even if the home office is experiencing a total power or connectivity blackout.

2   **Commoditized endpoints are instantly replaceable** - Because user devices are *gateways* to services instead of *hosts*, the failure or loss of a device should have minimal impact on the user. With remote wipe capabilities and a quick update to user credentials, stolen devices can be rendered completely inert. If a traveling user's computer is destroyed, everything the user needs can be brought up immediately on an alternate device. New off-the-shelf devices can be configured remotely in minutes, often with no involvement by IT.

3   **Onboarding, role changes, and exiting is simple and powerful** - With a single digital identity tying everything together, user access to all systems, applications, and services is easy to track and can be instantly disabled. This drastically reduces the risk of a former employee retaining unauthorized access to systems. Tools from vendors including OneLogin and BetterCloud can automate

---

[23]http://www.datacenterknowledge.com/archives/2012/10/30/major-flooding-nyc-data-centers/

cloud application permissions based on job roles, reducing IT workload while making true least-privilege programmatic and simple to maintain.

4 **Control of what matters** - Rather than digging through system logs and monitoring server statuses, Ultralight focuses on monitoring user activity across the spectrum of the organization's services. This is a higher and more business-relevant level of visibility, enabling enforceable controls built around user behavior. It is possible to detect a credit card number shared inappropriately in real time, monitor third party tools, and block unauthorized or unnecessary applications.

In 2015, Information Week identified six reasons why cloud security would eventually beat local datacenter security[24]. The list included big-data threat intelligence, certificate management, malware detection with retroactive healing, continuous updates with latest-threat mitigation, end-to-end visibility, and robust denial-of-service protection.

While some of these can be achieved on the local network, doing so is costly, complex, and time-consuming. And comprehensive threat intelligence and denial-of-service protection is simply impossible for most small businesses on the scale that Google, Amazon, or Microsoft can provide it.

---

[24]http://www.informationweek.com/cloud/infrastructure-as-a-service/why-cloud-security-beats-your-data-center/d/d-id/1321354

Hardware-Minimizing

Why we suffered with Internet Explorer all those years

When Microsoft created Internet Explorer to challenge Netscape back in the '90s, it wasn't because the company saw a new revenue opportunity. Rather, Microsoft understood that Internet-based web applications could make traditional operating systems irrelevant. Being the dominant operating system developer, Microsoft felt this undesirable.

Steve Ballmer said 20 years ago, "We look at [Navigator] as a very direct threat for Windows if we don't do a good job. That's not a threat a month from now or five months from now. It's a longer-term threat, but it's a clear threat. It's sort of an everyday issue, but if we screw up, you won't know for a few years."[25]

Microsoft succeeded. Netscape was destroyed (for which Netscape itself bears much responsibility), and Windows and Internet Explorer dominated market share for a decade. This dominance made them the de facto standard, allowing Microsoft to stall the rise of robust, cross-platform web applications. The release of Internet Explorer 6 in 2001 ushered in the browser dark ages, a period of stagnating capability, poor interoperability, and atrocious security.[26]

Microsoft's position on industry standards in 2001 was clear. A Microsoft technical evangelist explained, "Microsoft will look at each

---

[25]http://www.cnet.com/news/ballmer-navigator-a-threat-to-windows/
[26]http://www.howtogeek.com/howto/32372/htg-explains-why-do-so-many-geeks-hate-internet-explorer/

standard individually and determine how important it is for the customer."[27] If this sounds a bit like Time Warner Cable explaining why most customers don't really want Gigabit Internet[28], there's a reason.

Internet Explorer 6 would serve as Microsoft's flagship browser for more than five years and remain the most commonly used browser until 2008[29]. During this period, Java, Flash, and other technologies attempted to reduce cross-platform compatibility challenges and enable robust web applications. None, however, would realize the potential of a truly web-based computer until Google's Chromebook appeared in 2011, fully 15 years after Ballmer's declaration.

Thankfully, the dark ages have passed and the realization of powerful, cloud-based web applications is upon us. Commoditization of the local operating system represents a massive change in how businesses can get work done, a change that has been long anticipated, long pursued, and, for some, long feared. Ultralight embraces this commoditization, focusing on the browser and cross-platform apps to get work done on whichever device best suits the user.

If a piece of hardware can empower an employee, connect to the Internet, and be adequately secured, that is all that matters[30]. By abstracting away the underlying system, tech capabilities can be *built*

---

[27]https://msdn.microsoft.com/en-us/library/bb263979(v=vs.85).aspx
[28]http://www.theverge.com/2013/2/27/4036128/time-warner-cable-no-consumer-demand-for-fiber-gigabit-internet
[29]https://www.w3counter.com/trends
[30]http://www.techradar.com/us/news/computing/pc/taking-the-business-world-by-storm-the-rise-of-google-s-chromebook-1258553

to the browser to assemble an integrated set of apps that are available cross-platform with minimal management overhead.

This commoditization is what Microsoft vigorously opposed back in 1996, and what so many technology companies are still trying to avoid today. A great many of the challenges regular businesses face are inspired by this conflict between simple accessibility and hardware dependency. With Ultralight, there is no conflict - if it's not trivially accessible cross-platform, it isn't Ultralight.

Simplify the local network

The local network is for the Internet, the Internet isn't for the local network.

Use the minimum network structure necessary to be stable and secure. Generally, if users can reliably access the Internet quickly, the hardware is sufficient. If admin, business, and guest access are segregated, the structure is probably sufficient. If the firewall is blocking and reporting malware-spreading and other unlawful activity, security is sufficient.[31]

Smaller organizations rarely need dozens of subnets or VLANS, and sophisticated network management is a distraction from higher value activities. With Ultralight, little of importance should reside on the local network anyway. That means switches don't have to be smart, they have to be fast. Look for quick, reliable, inexpensive switches that can be setup with essentially identical configurations. Use spanning-

---

[31]The security key here is *and reporting* - no amount of automated network security will substitute for rapid, effective response when an issue does arise.

tree protocol (STP), keep a spare pre-configured device, and move on to more important things.

With regard to network security, use the simplest configuration necessary to protect critical system interfaces and shape traffic. Where possible, use identical configurations across switches to keep setup, maintenance, and replacement simple. For those systems that must operate onsite, identify and document a clear security baseline for each system type. Actually implement and maintain the baseline.

The universal, expendable endpoint

With Ultralight operations, the endpoint (the computer, tablet, or smart device) that employees use becomes much less important. It matters primarily as a gateway, not a destination, which means it can be easily replaced on the fly. A catastrophic local hardware failure should have minimal impact on the user - simply swap out the device, log in, and continue working.

This applies across Windows, macOS, Linux, Android, iOS, and Chrome. It should be possible to run a small business entirely on Android tablets, for instance, with only minor modifications to workflows. There are a number of reasons this might be undesirable, but it is trivial to facilitate technologically.

For smaller organizations, a more practical benefit is that it enables simple, robust integration of Apple's macOS and Google's Chromebooks. Both offer similar functionality to a classic Windows-based PC, but with their own distinct advantages.

Google's Chromebooks are shockingly secure[32,33] and incredibly simple. As an admin, the difference between managing a Chromebook and managing a Windows PC is the difference between *driving* and *building* a car, respectively. The catch is that classic Windows-only programs don't run on Chromebooks, including the traditional Office Suite. To the degree a small business can adopt Google Docs or the web-based Office 365, Chromebooks can be a powerful way to increase security, bring simplicity, and save money.

While Chromebooks will have value for some businesses, there are many tasks they can't yet perform. For staff who must still handle complex local workloads, Ultralight makes it possible to easily deploy and support Apple's macOS. When IBM deployed more than 50,000 Mac systems in 2014, they discovered that end users had far fewer problems. Whereas 40% of Windows PC users needed to ask for help, only 5% of Mac users had similar issues. IBM discovered, "the incremental purchase price of a Mac pays for itself several times over the life of the device."[34]

Ultralight makes it possible to choose endpoints based on what benefits users need most, not what a particular software package requires or legacy management tool demands. Some environments may have a variety of endpoint systems represented together. That's okay. Ultralight allows IT to focus on authentication and security[35], leaving the rest for the browser (or mobile apps) to handle.

---

[32]http://www.computerworld.com/article/2475853/cybercrime-hacking/a-chromebook-offers-defensive-computing-when-traveling.html
[33]http://dhanus.mit.edu/docs/ChromeOSSecurity.pdf
[34]http://bgr.com/2015/10/15/mac-vs-pc-ibm/
[35]More details about how this can be done are included in Part 3

Finally, while not specifically related to Ultralight, there is one other endpoint observation I'm compelled to mention. If you're part of a small business trying to save every penny, it is important to understand that cheap computers don't save money. Ever. Low quality parts, inadequate configurations, bloatware, and poor service compound to steal much more time and money than you'll pay simply giving users great devices for getting work done.

Instead, buy business class PCs or Chromebooks with strong configurations and built with quality parts. Or, as we discussed above, consider Apple's Mac lineup. This will make life easier for both IT and users, increasing productivity while reducing maintenance and repair costs. Over the life of a computer, the premium for a high-quality product is typically pennies a day.

BYOD, COPE and other acronyms

The tech world is awash in acronyms trying to describe the ownership and usage relationships between employees and technology. BYOD stands for "bring your own device", where employees use a personal device for business functions. COPE stands for "corporately owned, personally enabled", where the business owns the device but allows employees to use it for both business and personal functions. Ultralight can work well with both, but it is important to understand the differences between them.

When discussed in technical circles, BYOD and COPE typically refer to mobile devices - smartphones and tablets. For smaller organizations, however, many traditional computers will fall into this category. In nearly every small business I've encountered (and some medium businesses), leaders used their personal computers to accomplish critical business functions.

Whatever approach the organization chooses, it must take into account the full spectrum of current usage. This is critical to achieve visibility and security, as well as to ensure IT can support employees effectively.

As a nonprofit, the conventional wisdom at our service desk had been, "make whatever we have work." Consequently, we ended up spending most of our time repairing older, personally-owned computers. When we actually started measuring the time we spend maintaining crummy systems, we realized how truly wasteful this was. It didn't just destroy the productivity of the service desk. It was reducing the productivity of our *entire* workforce. We were taking a moderate but measurable cost - the cost to deploy a good computer to a user - and turning it into a massive hidden cost in the form of lost productivity and added service desk workload.

We discovered the cost to deploy quality endpoints, whether Windows or Mac, is a fraction of the cost we would have paid in lost productivity if we didn't. Ultimately, we found a combination of BYOD for mobile (using Google App's built in MDM) and COPE (for traditional systems) provided greater security and service, happier staff, and the highest financial value.

When capabilities are managed to the browser, maintaining a broad array of systems in a BYOD or COPE environment is straightforward.

With tools like OneLogin and JumpCloud, authentication can be managed across apps and systems regardless of ownership. With a handful of small but powerful security tools integrated as well, we were able to secure, monitor, and manage both corporately and personally owned mobile and traditional systems entirely from the cloud.

Enclave legacy systems and services

Ultralight is a framework for decision-making, not a silver bullet for every problem. Some challenges will require onsite servers, full-stack deployments, and legacy software or services. Others will take time before an Ultralight solution can be effectively deployed. In those instances, the goal should be to enclave legacy systems and services to the greatest degree possible.

When I first began exploring these ideas, my team and I had little choice. Our existing technology stack was a Jenga puzzle of obscure dependencies. To untangle the mess, we first had to clarify what we had, identify what we could move to the cloud, and find ways to do it without breaking anything.

Some local systems were easy to completely remove. Others took more time, and a few proved irreplaceable (such as print servers). Calendars were very easy - a few imports and exports, and our users suddenly had vastly more capability and collaborative power. Moving off our legacy email platform, however, took multiple stages.

We gently moved the backend first, allowing users to continue to connect using their existing clients. This allowed us to transition off our old servers without impacting in a substantial way how users conducted daily operations. Once the backend migration was complete, we began educating users on the power of web-based operations, and eventually made the web interface the organization's standard.

Moving to Google Drive was more complex still. Some workloads, particularly in our Finance department, were built around the capabilities of a Windows-based file server. This is where enclaving was critical. We didn't stop migrating to Drive, but we did continue to support the specific workflow of that department on a local server. As we learned how to master Drive, we updated the department's processes and were eventually able to migrate it to Drive as well.

Where calendars took us a few days, completing the move to Drive took the better part of 18 months. Throughout our migrations, we learned to build momentum with quick wins, enclave challenge points, identify and test options, and finally implement solutions.

For the servers we couldn't remove, we focused instead on reducing user exposure. Our initial goal was to make it so users never had to interact directly with local systems. Our final goal was to ensure that a local server failure would never impede user productivity.

The datacenter that isn't

While Ultralight is focused first on replacing commodity infrastructure, I can't leave the broader topic of cloud compute entirely untouched. It is cheaper than ever to leverage cloud-based capabilities to underpin custom applications and indispensable server workloads.

Google Cloud Computer, Amazon Web Services, and Microsoft Azure make it possible to move the entire datacenter to a platform that provides tremendous flexibility and scale. With an Ultralight infrastructure approach already in place, authentication and management of these services should be seamless.

The nuances of full cloud-based or hybrid-cloud datacenter operations are beyond the scope of this book, but it is important to understand what is possible. The key is minimizing the need to manage hardware, regardless of the form it takes. Every physical system the organization can offload liberates time, resources, and expertise.

Change Management

How an organization implements change and provide support is as important as the technologies it uses. The perfect Ultralight platform will struggle to provide value if users aren't educated and bought-in.

The IT department must transition from being "the people you deal with when stuff breaks" to a trusted internal team of business enablers. It needs to become the first place people turn to for ideas, not the last place they go when there are no other options.

IT must be excellent. But it doesn't usually start there.

Starting from the bottom

As a new IT manager, I had zero influence beyond my department. IT had been a black hole, and no one in the organization trusted us to fix their printers, never mind speak into business processes or manage major change initiatives. We knew that moving to Google Apps for Work would enable us to drastically improve the quality of our services, but there were major roadblocks.

Executive leaders wanted IT to function better, but there was no plan, and there would be no formal support for specific initiatives. When we presented our proposal for Google Apps, the leadership was skeptical we could complete so large a project amid the quagmire. Still, anything was better than the status quo, and they gave us permission to proceed.

Without deliberate executive sponsorship for our initiatives, we wouldn't have the authority to enforce changes with the rest of the organization's leadership. And we couldn't build a strong coalition around our vision, because IT hadn't yet earned anyone's trust. They didn't want to waste their time with us. It didn't matter how good we made the idea sound, leaders wouldn't take a chance on IT until they knew we could execute.

This created a chicken-and-egg dilemma where we needed to successfully implement change to build trust, and we needed trust to initiate change. Our question became, "How do you drive change when you have the responsibility but don't have sponsorship, a coalition, or authority?" We needed a change management strategy.

So my team and I worked out an approach we called *Change Management by Osmosis.*

Change Management by Osmosis

We needed to build trust and initiate change simultaneously, so we started at the one place we actually had some control: *new users.* They had no history to unlearn, and no habits to break. We tried to make their initial experience with IT as awesome as possible, and we put them on on our cloud-based platform instead of the legacy systems. At first, we didn't talk about all the sophisticated new capabilities it contained. We were just laying the foundation, building rapport and expanding the base of cloud users.

Second, we identified **tech-savvy leaders** who met two criteria:

1.   They understood intuitively the value of what we were trying to do. This meant they didn't have to trust us to buy into Google Apps. In fact, our attempting the migration *increased* their confidence in us as they realized we really wanted to make things better.

2.   They led teams with relatively uncomplicated needs. We needed to learn how to execute well, and complex use-cases weren't the right place to start. These teams helped us develop and refine our processes, giving us the knowledge and experience we'd need to win over more wary leaders down the line.

These tech-savvy leaders were critical to bootstrapping our coalition mid-flight, and in helping us develop the techniques that would be crucial to Ultralight operations down the road.

Third, we went after **low-hanging fruit**. Typically, these were major pain points with easy fixes, the classic easy-wins. When a user would arrive exasperated with our legacy email system, we'd explain the capabilities of our new system and offer to switch them. When we discovered one department couldn't coordinate between their managers and their staff because of a convoluted calendaring system, we demonstrated Google Calendar and offered to migrate them all to Apps.

These wins helped build trust while driving us towards the critical mass required to get the full collaboration value from Apps. As more users encountered and used Apps, more users wanted to. We didn't have a hard schedule (though we carefully tracked our progress), and we didn't force anyone to switch. Instead, we relied on osmosis with gentle encouragement. We didn't generally go to users insisting they change; they came to us and asked to be upgraded.

But there was nothing passive about our effort: it was a deliberate, exhaustive soft-sell. Internally, we were aggressively looking for best practices and refining our processes. Across the organization, we were actively selling capabilities, educating leaders and users, and testing new use cases.

Our watershed moment came when a reluctant leader, sensing impending change, attempted to enlist executive sponsorship to *stop* our migration (this illuminated for me why executive sponsorship is so important, and should serve as a warning about the limits of change management by osmosis). This incident gave us the opportunity to demonstrate to leadership the benefits we were already realizing in the organization, with case-by-case examples.

To undermine our effort, this reluctant leader had raised concerns about security. So we addressed it directly. Breaking down the organization's digital security posture across classic confidentiality, integrity, and availability lines, we addressed 22 critical security issues that moving to Google Apps would improve or resolve. We left with full executive sponsorship and the authority necessary to integrate the last corners of the organization.

Change management by osmosis was our solution to a specific challenge - how to leverage change to build credibility. It helped us pull ourselves up by our bootstraps and build momentum in a situation where we had very little trust or authority. If you're already part of a high performance IT culture with strong support within your organization, great! If your situation is more like ours, however, I hope you find something useful in our osmosis experience.

Part 3: Deploying Ultralight (A Google Apps Guide)

Why Google Apps?

This chapter deals extensively with Google Apps for Work and the systems and ideas that can make it powerful for smaller organizations. I focus on Google Apps for two reasons. First, Ultralight requires a centralized, cloud-based platform like Apps. Second, Google Apps is what I have the most experience with. Ultralight concepts are not bound to Google Apps, but the only other mainstream option at the time of printing is Microsoft Office 365.

In the following sections I mention a number of specific tools. My mention of these tools is informed by my personal experience as an IT manager. There are no paid endorsements in this book. If I mention a tool, it's because my team and I encountered it, and I thought it would be useful for others to know what we learned.

In straddling the gap between the science and art of technology implementation, I've tried to combine important concepts with personal experiences and direct applications. My experiences describe one way to implement Ultralight with Google Apps - but there are certainly more ways to continue building on innovative technologies. I encourage you to pursue them.

My conviction is that technologies emerging today can empower businesses in remarkable ways, but only if we shift from the Second Platform approach we've been using for forty years. Tomorrow's businesses will have lighter, more user-centered technology, and they'll be faster, more productive, and more secure as a consequence. My hope is that the experiences described here help you along that path regardless of which platform you choose.

Google Apps as a Foundation for Ultralight

Google Apps for Work fits Ultralight from the start. It requires no local servers or datacenter hardware. Authentication, email, contacts, calendar, file sharing, video conferencing, and messaging are all embedded into a single cloud-based product. A basic router is sufficient to connect an office with Google Apps.

This enables IT to move away from managing servers and datacenter infrastructure, drastically reducing capital costs and the need for legacy administrators. As of this writing, Ultralight (to the extent described here) has only been possible for a few years. When I mention specific products, they may be one of the only products that offer the integrated capabilities needed to execute a truly Ultralight deployment.

The quality and number of suitable products and services continue to grow rapidly, however, and interested organizations should research the latest available options. I've included an appendix at the end of this book with a number of technology accelerators for your reference. It is by no means a complete list, but it should serve as a useful point of departure for further investigation.

A Word of Caution

My first foray with Google Apps was catastrophic. It was 2008, and Apps was newly hatched. I was doing IT work on the side while completing my degree, and agreed to help a small business upgrade their infrastructure. I foolishly believed that my consumer experience with Google products gave me the expertise to start upending business processes I didn't fully understand.

I was wrong. Most employees had been there for the better part of a decade. They all worked in the same office, they didn't care about mobility, and they loved using Outlook. When I brought in Google Apps, it broke nearly everything they knew, and they didn't care about any of its new capabilities.

The reality is that some organizations will experience minimal lift from the Ultralight approach. Consider if:

1   Your employees use mainly proprietary software that *require* legacy tools (this organization depended on Microsoft Access)
2   You don't foresee any significant infrastructure upgrades
3   No one works remotely or on mobile devices
4   Your current platform is trivially maintainable
5   You don't anticipate meaningful turnover or growth

...then you should carefully consider whether or not Google Apps will be worth the effort.

Next, you should be aware Google Apps isn't perfect. It had problems in 2008, and it has problems now. As of this writing, Drive is not an enterprise-class file management product on its own (more on how to resolve that later). Cloud Print is still experimental, and Sites is an aesthetic abomination. And if you regularly work with highly sensitive information, you'll need to take some special precautions.

But whether you're bootstrapping a startup or you're in a growing organization approaching the next major infrastructure upgrade, Google Apps can provide remarkable value as the core of an Ultralight deployment. It allows even a small IT shop to build a robust, sustainable, and highly scalable technology platform in a fraction of the time and for a fraction of the cost of legacy technologies.

Make Google Authentication Ubiquitous

Users should only need one login to do everything they do. Google Apps handles the core collaboration tools, but each organization will have its own requirements that demand third-party functionality. When searching for additional functionality, consider:

1. **Existing products may already authenticate through Google**. Once everyone is onboard with Apps, products that are already in use in the organization may be able to authenticate through Apps. Take advantage of this capability to simplify user management.

2. **Google Authentication should be a requirement for new services**. Ultralight is about a simple, unified experience. Having an unmanageable array of best-in-class products will result in a below-average user IT experience. If a product or service doesn't integrate with Apps, explore a reliable alternative that does.

3. **Integrating Google Authenticating with custom applications is really, really easy**. If the organization is developing its own web applications, providing authentication through Apps is an easy win for IT and the staff.

Administrators will inevitably be responsible for managing separate and secure logins for the various products, services, and systems the organization needs. Users, however, should have as streamlined an experience as possible.

One of the final changes we made when deploying Apps was integrating Google authentication into our custom web services. This improved a number of internal processes for IT while simplifying access for our users. It also ensured the security measures we enforced in Apps cascaded to our web applications.

Use Google Chrome
(and drop local email and calendar clients)

Our environment originally had no less than five distinct email clients in use when I arrived, including Outlook, Thunderbird, Entourage,

Live Mail, and Mac Mail. Mac users were on an isolated calendaring system, and more than half of our PC users had no organizational calendar access at all. Our small IT team was swamped managing the constant conflicts and idiosyncratic behaviors of these applications.

We knew that Google Apps would provide a unified backend for email and calendaring, which we needed. But we also knew we could do more. As we migrated to Google Apps, we installed the Chrome Browser on every system and began educating users on the features unique to Gmail and Google Calendar when used through Chrome.

To demonstrate how the unified web experience could save time, we showed them a basic scheduling workflow in Chrome where users could:

- get corporate contact information from Gmail
- use that contact information to send an email
- automatically include email recipients in a new Calendar event
- find the best time by instantly viewing participant availability
- schedule conference rooms simultaneously
- embed files for reference, keeping everyone on the same page
- use built-in video calling to enable face-to-face conversations

When used through the browser, Google Apps tools work together to provide a level of integration and real-time collaboration that is very difficult to achieve with legacy client applications. These capabilities are central to the user-centered experience, and work best through the browser.

With Ultralight, the goal should be to eliminate dependence on local client applications entirely. To do that, the browser - not the computer - takes the management focus.

Manage to the browser

Managing to the browser makes life easier for users and IT staff. In our environment, we no longer fix a failed computer while the user waits. Instead, we give them a fresh computer, and they go back to work immediately. We repair their old computer as we have time, and then make it available as a warm spare for the next failure. This is endpoint commoditization, and it ensures that users always have the resources they need to get work done.

For this reason, the Google Chrome browser is the single most powerful tool IT has to simplify endpoints. Along with Google mobile applications on portable devices, it ensures that any Internet connected device can become a functional work platform with minimal IT effort. IT no longer manages computers in the cumbersome Second Platform sense. Rather, IT secures computers and manages Chrome.

When users log into the Chrome browser with their Apps account, they get access to every individual setting, bookmark, and extension they use. They also get every user policy established in the Chrome Management portion of the Apps Admin console. These policies include pushing (or restricting) extensions, making the home button point to the organization's intranet portal, and managing additional security and customization features.

Any computer with Chrome, regardless of ownership or location, can be a conduit to the users' customized work environment. This takes much of the pain out of bring-your-own-device (BYOD), and allows a flexible corporately-owned personally-enabled (COPE) strategy. This also greatly reduces the challenge of integrating new technology platforms.

If software requires anything more than a login to configure for a local machine, get rid of it. When endpoints are freed from cumbersome client applications:

1. **Users depend on their Apps identity, not a specific computer**. Because they get their work done through Chrome, they get exactly the same user experience on any platform with Chrome - their digital identity, not the physical system, is the key.

2. **All data remains in the cloud**, so critical user data is not bound to a single computer or preconfigured set of devices. Email and calendar data is never lost with a failed or stolen system, and users are free to access all their data from any platform.

3. **Any platform that will run Chrome is sufficient to get work done**. This reduces endpoint management requirements to tracking and securing, and makes BYOD and COPE trivially maintainable. It also ends the Mac versus PC debate.

4. **IT supports a single product on all endpoints: the Chrome browser**. There is no need to troubleshoot an array of client applications or fight cross-platform client compatibility issues. IT

transitions from a break-fix relationship with client applications to an educational role teaching users how to get the most from Chrome.

Removing customized client applications and managing to Chrome is a critical first step in the Ultralight process. It eliminates dependence on the endpoint. The next step is to eliminate dependence on the local network, and that usually starts with the file server.

Use Google Drive with AODocs (and drop the local file server)

Local file servers are the opposite of Ultralight. Local file servers require hardware. They require local authentication, VPNs for remote access, server administration, backups, backups of backups, physical security, and more. Ultralight means moving the entire file management system to the cloud. Or rather, to Google Drive.

Drive is a product that builds momentum. If users are indoctrinated in the ways of the local file server, the real benefits of Drive will take time to percolate through the organization. And that's OK. But to achieve long-term success, IT must overcome a few challenges to make Drive a comprehensive solution. It can be done, and it is worth it.

Strengths and weaknesses in Drive

Drive is all about the user. Users can access their files anywhere and control who else can access them. It is cloud-based, requiring zero hardware to support or maintain. And it can be operated entirely through a browser or mobile app, eliminating dependence on custom system configurations.

Drive has matured tremendously in the past few years, and now includes the ability to read and write Microsoft Office files with considerable fidelity. The Drive Client has become more robust, and the web interface has become faster, simpler, and more intuitive.

Still, on its own, Drive has substantial flaws that can make it impractical as the core file management tool for some organizations. Thankfully, these flaws have readily available fixes that fit well with Ultralight. To successfully deploy Drive as the primary file management platform, IT must address three challenges: permissions, legacy file conflicts, and very large files.

The Drive permissions problem

Google Drive file permissions are so extremely user-focused, they are very difficult to manage organizationally. This may not be an issue if users are tech savvy, the organization doesn't require structured file management, or you have a small, stable team. For the rest of us, it can be a real problem. This is why: every file you create belongs to you, no matter what folder you create it in and no matter how those folders are managed.   (If you're familiar with the perils of this implementation, you can skip right to the next section about redemption)

Consider Drive's default behavior. If you create a file in the _Accounting_ folder, it continues to belong to you when you leave Accounting and transfer to Marketing. Even after you can no longer access the

Accounting folder, you still own the file and can modify or destroy it. Being removed from *Accounting* will orphan the file in your Drive, though. Orphaned means even though you still control it, you don't actually see it anymore. You have to search for it specifically.

This is not particularly intuitive or secure, and it leads to curious behavior when you, say, leave the organization. If the administrator destroys your account without transferring ownership of your files, *every file you've ever created in any folder will be destroyed,* including in *Accounting*. This may come as an unpleasant surprise to the CFO.

If the administrator instead transfers ownership of your files to your new colleague in Marketing, they will suddenly have access to ALL your files, including all the financial data you owned from your Accounting days. And if the Marketing colleague then deletes all the excess Accounting files they think they don't need, they are actually destroying live files from the *Accounting* folder. Again, undesirable.

Worst of all, if your colleague in Marketing is given legitimate access to *Accounting*, they will end up with two identical (essentially symbolically linked) instances of the same file. Offering this scenario to your users is like releasing kittens into a minefield. An undesirable outcome is inevitable.

There are manual workarounds to some of Drive's permission challenges, but they all depend on making end users do nerdy things. None of these workarounds address the root issue: the complex *user-ownership* approach in Drive is not actually *user-centered* in a holistic sense. Drive's folder permission propagation is counterintuitive, and requires the user to do more and know more than they ought to. In a business environment, most users expect folder location to inform file ownership, period.

File management redemption with AODocs

The permissions challenge in Drive can be solved, and AODocs is the most robust solution available today. AODocs integrates with Google Drive to create true organizational folders.[36] This is precisely what is needed to resolve many of the issues that arise from a vanilla Drive instance.

Whenever users create files in an AODocs managed folder, file ownership is automatically transferred to a service account. Files saved in a departmental folder behave the way you'd expect on a traditional file server. This largely resolves the permission problems previously described.

AODocs returns real folder management to leaders and IT staff without compromising the Ultralight benefits of the Drive platform. It also provides the core security features you would expect with business-class file management in the cloud. Folder structures are locked down, with sharing restricted based on department and user. Files in the Accounting folder, for instance, can be restricted to current department members only, while the Marketing folders may allow sharing with outside organizations.

---

[36]AODocs is a third party Apps integration created to enable "The power of Enterprise Document Management with the ease of use of Google Drive." https://www.aodocs.com/

AODocs is a compromise. In exchange for enhanced control, it can limit some of the fluid sharing users are familiar with in Drive. The good news is that you can use AODocs libraries alongside traditional folder shares in Drive, affording the best of both worlds. And AODocs provides different levels of control, from unobtrusive re-permissioning to strict lockdowns.

AODocs also helps solve the second major Drive challenge: version conflicts with legacy files.

Locking down file conflicts

In the real world, you aren't likely to escape the reach of Microsoft Office. Too many organizations use it and will continue to use it, and you need to collaborate with them. That means using Office files in Drive.

With traditional document files, only one user may edit the file at a time. If the document is on a classic file server, once the first user opens the document, the file is locked. Additional users will be unable to open the document for editing until it is closed, unlocking the file. This mechanism ensures users don't accidentally overwrite each other's data.

Traditional files stored in Drive do not have this locking feature. It is possible for your users to have a dozen instances of the same Office document open simultaneously on different computers. If all users save their changes at the same time, Google will simultaneously receive a dozen different versions of the same file. There is no way to automatically integrate these file versions, so Google will create a separate "conflict" file for each irreconcilable version and let you sort it out. In my limited experience, sorting it out sucks.

AODocs includes a fix for this. It adds functionality to Drive in Chrome where legacy file types are automatically "checked out" when the user opens the file. When the user saves and closes the document, the file is updated in Drive and checked back in, enabling write access for other users. Like a classic file server.

Managing very large files

Drive attempts to abstract away the distance between your physical device and the data you store and share through Drive. You can pretend your data is everywhere, all the time, because it mostly behaves that way.

Your Drive data is actually really far away, relying on countless lower level systems in use by a whole bunch of other people. No amount of programming will change that, and sometimes the technical limitations of TCP/IP will "leak" through to your Drive experience.

And Drive leaks most obviously when dealing with massive files. Long uploads and downloads can be confusing for users trying to work collaboratively with a legacy file type. And if multiple users have the same large file shared through the Drive client, a midday file update can result in massive network congestion. To address this, IT needs a strategy for handling very large files.

The single best way to manage very large files in Drive is to move to Austin, Texas and get Google Fiber. For the rest of us, there are three more practical ways to mitigate the problem.

Reduce dependence on large files. Ultralight is about removing unnecessary complexity, and part of that process involves breaking data into usable, accessible chunks. Those old 500 page PDF images from Human Resources? Might be time to do some optical character recognition and convert them to a lighter, more indexable format.

A few of our departments discovered they could replace large traditional spreadsheets with Google Sheets. Converting these files made them lighter, more accessible, and more collaborative.

Ensure the network is amazing by taking some of Ultralight's cost savings and reinvesting in bandwidth. In one environment, we increased raw download speed almost 1,100% at the headquarters without increasing our infrastructure services budget.

Enclave special cases. The Marketing department may have no way around working with massive video files, and IT must be able to support them. Look for simple, elegant ways to support special cases. A network storage device that provides local network access but uploads changes to Drive in the evening, for instance, is a straightforward way to solve the problem while still generating value from Drive as the core platform (in this case, for backup).

Google Docs are worth it

There are a number of competitive products in the cloud storage arena that will plug into Apps, so why Google Drive?

In addition to its high level of integration with the rest of the Apps suite, Google Drive includes Google Docs. If you haven't experimented with a Google Sheet yet, you need to stop what you're doing and test one with multiple users connected simultaneously. It is an amazing set of capabilities, and most business don't realize how powerful it can be.

Users work together with real-time data in a simple, cloud-based environment that builds on their legacy skills. The challenges of getting access, managing file types, coordinating input, and deconflicting duplicate data are eliminated. These qualities enable simple, elegant solutions to classic problems.

In our environment, Sheets (and its *importrange* function) actually let us replace an entire custom reporting system[37]. We used this ability to pool important information from a dozen countries around the world simultaneously, giving us a light, robust reporting tool that functioned in real-time. This solution replaced traditional spreadsheets, a project management platform, and countless hours of tedious data entry and manipulation.

With AODocs, Drive becomes a viable enterprise file management platform. But it is Docs that turns Drive into a truly indispensable collaboration tool.

---

[37] The *importrange* function enables a Google Sheet to pull data from any other Google Sheet.

Use Voice or Dialpad
(and drop onsite telephony)

In the United States, Google will give you a 10-digit number *for free* through Google Voice. This integrates with Google Hangouts, and includes a number of features including texting, forwarding to multiple devices, and voice-to-text messaging. It is an amazing capability available at no cost, and it integrates transparently into the Apps environment. As soon as your users log into Chrome, they can begin making and receiving calls using Hangouts.

The snag is that there are exactly zero business management features native to Google Voice. Want to set up a main number and route to call groups, or manage your user's Voice accounts from the Admin panel? Tough. You can't. Further, you may not be able to get a Google Voice number with your preferred area code, and there are times when none may be available at all (Google maintains a pool of available numbers and periodically replenishes them).

Enter the Grasshopper

Google doesn't include business management for Voice, but you can bring business management to Google. With a bit of elbow grease on setup, Voice numbers can be used alongside a service like Grasshopper.

Grasshopper is a cloud solution that provides a "virtual" main number and overlays many of the management features you'd expect from a true business phone system. This is an inexpensive and flexible way to provide voice services, particularly for smaller teams. And there is no hardware to manage or maintain.

There are limitations. When using Voice to make calls, users must pay for international calls with their individual Google Wallet accounts. IT can't centrally enable international calling or have the charges post to a single account. IT also can't track calls in a single place for analytics purposes, which makes this a non-starter for serious call center activities. This configuration doesn't allow classic desk phones either - users must have an existing smartphone or tablet to run the Hangouts and Grasshopper apps, or be tied to their computer for voice services.

In some environments, this will not be practical. Many organizations need at least a few physical desk phones, and call centers require more robust management and reporting. There's an Ultralight solution for that too.

Unified Communication with Dialpad

The real gem of Apps-based telephony is Dialpad. Dialpad is what Voice should have been in Google Apps for Work.

Administrators centrally manage users within an Apps domain, assigning 10-digit extensions (so everyone has their own direct line) and adding call routing as necessary. International billing is centrally managed, and physical phones integrate seamlessly. A Chrome extension provides softphone capabilities, and users can configure routing, voicemail, text, and other functions through the browser.

Dialpad has flaws. Reporting is still a work in progress, and traditional deskphone capabilities are rudimentary. You can make and receive calls from desk phones, but all the real power is in the browser. Dialpad is meant to be used through Chrome, and that is where (like most Ultralight services) it is most powerful.

Still, products like Dialpad point to the future of business communication.

Use Sites
(and drop the local intranet site)

Sites has languished in the Google inventory as focus shifted to other products, but it still provides essential functionality. It is the simplest way to replace the classic intranet portal, it is straightforward to manage, and it is completely Ultralight.

The key is *simple*. Sites, while unglamorous, is still as smooth as a Lexus compared to Sharepoint's backhoe-loader levels of gratuitous complexity. For organizations looking to get from point A to point B on their intranet, Sites is easy to access and manage. And for smaller organizations, this is enough.

Use Cloud-Based Endpoint Management
(and drop Active Directory)

Google Apps provides a user-centered digital identity, allowing IT to use that identity to manage a range of classic user and intranet services. With Chromebooks, endpoint management is contained in Apps as well, providing true end-to-end control.

In the Apps Admin panel, IT has tremendous power over Chromebooks and how they are used. Chromebooks are far and away the most simple and secure platform for Apps-based organizations. As more applications become web-enabled or entirely cloud-based, there will be fewer and fewer reasons to deploy traditional Windows and macOS computers.

In addition to Chromebooks, Google Apps provides mobile device management (MDM) for Android and iOS. MDM features include device assignment, tracking, password and encryption policies, and remote wipe. This feature set has grown tremendously over the past 18 months, and should continue to develop.

However, if employees need classic applications requiring a traditional install on Windows or macOS, Chromebooks and mobile devices won't be sufficient. To fully support these systems in an Ultralight environment, IT must be able to provide Windows and macOS management as well.

In the shadows of IT

When we first started untangling our network, we realized less than a quarter of the systems we needed to support were actually connected to Active Directory. There were a number of reasons for this, including:

- About half our users relied on **personally owned computers**. This included executives and other senior leaders. IT had no management controls for these systems.

- Another third of our users were **remote with no local network access**. When users travelled, there was no enforceable VPN mechanism in place. Remote systems essentially disappeared from IT's control until users returned, which could be months.

- A smaller number of users were exclusively **iOS or Android tablet users, or Chromebook users**.

- Nearly all of our staff used **personal smartphones** to access corporate email.

We realized that AD would never (without enormous additional effort and investment) manage more than half of the systems we needed to support. Personally owned computers and BYOD mobile devices, at a minimum, would need a different solution. If we could find a solid solution for those outside systems that wasn't Active Directory, could we make it work for *all* our systems?

Cloud-based endpoint management assessment

With user services managed through the Chrome browser, there is little left to do on traditional endpoints. But those things are critically important. At a minimum, IT must be able to answer the following questions:

1. *What assets are you responsible for, and who is using them?* You need **user-centric asset management**. Google Apps will do this natively for mobile and Chrome devices, but traditional systems require something more.

2. *How will you provide administration and support remotely?* Ultralight frees users from the local network, which means IT must reach out to **administer and support systems wherever they are**.

3. *How will you secure corporate data?* Managing to the Chrome browser reduces the attack surface on endpoints, but it doesn't eliminate it. IT still needs to **provide baseline protections** to ensure against loss or theft, malware, and other endpoint-specific risks.

My team and I initially believed it would be straightforward to find a hosted tool that could address these three questions, but we were surprised by what we discovered when we began investigating further.

The problem is this: while *remote monitoring and management* (RMM) platforms offer many of these features, they are rarely Ultralight. They have high cost, high complexity, and assume integration with legacy onsite tools like Active Directory. Some are just for Windows, or just for macOS.

Few RMMs integrate with Apps, and most take a system-centric management view. Users are peripheral, making it difficult to centrally manage a user's experience across personal, corporate, mobile, and traditional devices. Finally, managing features and costs can range from cumbersome to bizarre, and the price tag can rise astronomically with feature set.

So we started looking for newer solutions. We wanted a system built for Google Apps that would give us the same controls on traditional computers that we had with mobile devices. Specifically, we wanted:

- LDAP, RADIUS, or similar authentication linked to Apps
- Asset management linking Apps users to systems
- Ability to control key security settings including password complexity, screen locking, system updates, and firewall configuration
- Remote support capability
- Compliance reporting

At that time, no single solution provided everything we wanted in a simple, elegant way. To solve our problem, we opted to combine the capabilities of a few products.

Deploying cloud-based endpoint management

The first was a user-focused, customizable, Apps-integrated asset management tool[38] that included robust service desk capabilities. It provided remote support, location tracking, and accountability. It became our database of record to track users, equipment, core infrastructure, and service desk operations.

The second was a directory-as-a-service tool[39] that enabled us to tie Google Apps to our systems for authentication as well as run configuration commands based on custom groups. In a field test, my team and I were able to use this tool to setup two-factor authentication on a corporate macOS system, implement WPA2 Enterprise security on our existing WiFi network using RADIUS, and tie it all back to our Google Apps directory for authentication. We had end-to-end authentication with a single set of credentials that didn't depend on the local network for anything but Internet access, and we did it all in less than an hour.

We had the ability to authenticate users across devices, networks, and services using a single digital identity. We could apply controls across mobile, traditional, personal, and corporate devices. And we could track, trend, and remotely connect to systems across our environment no matter where they were in the world.

This is the most efficient way we found to manage traditional endpoints with the least additional management overhead. I trust technology innovators will continue to push into this space and ultimately provide a single, simple tool to replace the three separate tools we ended up using. This effort is ongoing, and there are already

---

[38]https://www.samanage.com/
[39]https://jumpcloud.com/

additional tools available today that may prove useful. These are listed in the final section of this book, *Ultralight Enablers for Google Apps.*

Use Cloud-Based Endpoint Security
(and drop cumbersome antivirus suites)

A commoditized endpoint must be simple to use, maintain, and secure. Chromebooks provide this natively, but, as we discussed in the previous section, many organizations must still support some critical macOS or Windows applications. With cloud-based management, maintenance requirements are greatly reduced. What remains for traditional Windows and macOS computers is malware protection.

Since we first started looking for cloud-based antimalware solutions to fill this role, the segment has exploded. Nearly every major vendor has a cloud-managed product today, and these products range in features from simple malware detection to comprehensive endpoint security, auditing, and management.

Assess what you need, and get a product that does it without local infrastructure. The goal is to do the *important things* awesomely instead of trying to do *everything* with mediocrity. That means essential feature quality is far more important than raw feature quantity. Particularly with security products, there is always a new fear to sell. Resist the hype and find what makes the most sense for the organization's environment.

In our environment, what we needed most was buy-in. If we deployed a massive, cumbersome, or intrusive product, our users - starting with the CEO - would have simply insisted on having it removed. We reasoned having a competent product on every system was better security than having the *"perfect"* product on half of the systems.

We found a tool that met our requirements[40] and had considerable success in our initial deployment. It wasn't, however, truly Ultralight. It didn't integrate with our other management tools, and it was highly system-centric.

It did, however, get us closer to our goal. It freed us from one more server, and allowed us to support users everywhere without a VPN. The redundancy and management complexity it brought was substantially less than we had experienced with other products, and we were able to rapidly integrate it into our environment.

Use Google Cloud Print
(and best of luck to you...)

Let the naysaying Active Directory guru get their laughs here, because Google Cloud Print is challenging. It is not so difficult as to be unusable or to invalidate the rest of the paradigm, but it is definitely the most challenging product necessary to run Ultralight with Google Apps. Thankfully, it has been improving steadily, and should continue to do so.

---

[40]http://www.webroot.com/us/en/business

Cloud Print is amazing when properly configured and maintained. Users can print from any Chrome browser or Chrome device to any Internet-connected printer shared with them, anywhere. Cloud Print drivers are available for Windows as well, allowing users to print from other applications directly to a cloud printer.

Printer permissions are managed like every other resource in Apps, and Google Groups keeps management simple. I strongly recommend using a service account when linking printers to Cloud Print, as it will further simplify management and ensure user changes don't result in disappearing printers.

There is no doubt Cloud Print is how printing will work in the future. Right now, however, Cloud Print is still a beta product, and it has some issues IT staff need to be aware of.

1. **Keeping printers connected can be challenging** without a print server. Many vendors offer Cloud Print enabled printers, but we've struggled to find one that works consistently over an extended period. Changes to Cloud Print, outdated printer firmware, or network hiccups all serve to create problems.

In the end, we found installing the Google Cloud Print Service for Windows on a local print server is the most reliable way to use Cloud Print. It isn't pure Ultralight, but it's closer, and you still don't need Active Directory to manage printers.

2. **Print settings within Cloud Print are limited**, and users that regularly run complex print jobs or use specialized printers will need the capabilities provided by full printer drivers.

3. **macOS support is essentially nonexistent outside of Chrome.** There are a few apps that will allow printing to Cloud Print from the Print dialog, but they are not officially supported. The workaround for regular macOS applications is to print to PDF, move the PDF to Drive, and print from Drive in Chrome. It's not particularly elegant.

If staff are using Chromebooks, they need Cloud Print. Even if Chrome devices are not yet in the environment, Cloud Print is still a very powerful tool for managing basic printing needs. Fully supporting users, however, will likely require a hybrid implementation.

In our environment, we compromised by maintaining a print server to ensure reliable Cloud Print service. We also preconfiguring our high-volume multifunction printers as a baseline on all corporate systems. As Cloud Print continues to develop, we hope to drop these last vestiges of legacy infrastructure.

Notes on Security with Google Apps

Properly deployed, Google Apps can provide an incredibly robust set of protections from cyber threats. For a small organization, the depth and range of protections available through Apps would be prohibitively expensive to obtain from legacy technologies.

A few of App's security benefits include:

- **Protecting user accounts with two-step authentication** - Two-step authentication (using a USB key or other physical device to prove you are you) is a powerful way to stop keyloggers, phishing attacks, and malicious websites from compromising a user account. Google Apps makes this simple to enable and enforce for every user, providing an enormous level of user protection.

- **Backing up everything, all the time** - Cloud-to-cloud backup with products such as Backupify or Spanning ensure that all user data is immediately available in the event Google Apps experiences a catastrophic failure. More immediately relevant, it provides a high level of protection against accidental deletion by inattentive users. These systems allow users to self-recover lost data as well, reducing the demand for IT support.

- **File sharing and third-party app controls** - Tools like Cloudlock enable real-time monitoring of Drive sharing and can enforce actions when content sharing violations are detected. Cloudlock, BetterCloud and Google Apps' native interface provide a variety of controls to manage third-party app access to data, report on usage, and restrict privileges. AODocs, a file management tool, can turn Drive into a fully functional business file server with all the classic controls Windows administrators would expect.

- **End-to-end encryption** - Google now provides encrypted communication throughout their datacenters for much of their traffic (thanks Snowden!) Explicit, HIPAA-compliant encryption of Drive and GMail traffic is available through providers including CloudLock and Virtru, adding an additional layer of protection to business communications. Google's built-in MDM can force any mobile device touching business data to be fully encrypted before authorizing access. Chromebooks are only available fully encrypted.

Google Apps, like every technology platform, is not invincible. But for organizations looking for a solid platform that allows them to focus on the work before them, Apps provides a broad array of protections built in. What isn't available natively is available through a cadre of security-focused partners.

Master the Google Apps Domain

IT must master Google Apps to integrate it effectively in the organization. This includes understanding how it works, the limits of what it can do for users, and how other products and services integrate with it. IT staff should pursue the Google Apps Administrator certification and develop a test environment for experimentation. Waiting for the experts could mean waiting awhile - Apps is still young and changing fast, and the best way to learn is to dig into it.

With that said, there are a number of communities around Apps that may be helpful. Google provides their own, along with basic training resources. Google's own documentation seems restricted to *how* to use Apps. It has very little about what you should do or the broader *why* (otherwise I wouldn't need to write this). I have my own suspicions about why this is, but suffice it to say Google has remained reluctant to do more than show you your options.

To dig into best practices and the dialog surrounding Apps, there are a number of useful resources. They include:

BetterCloud Monitor

https://www.bettercloud.com/monitor/

BetterCloud's Monitor and Academy provide a variety of updates, guides, references, training, and data from the Google Apps world and the field of cloud computing generally.

Google for Work Connect

https://connect.googleforwork.com/

For current Google for Work admins, GWC provides a place to interact directly with Google, get the latest information, provide feedback or recommendations, and connect with other admins.

Google Apps Learning Center

http://learn.googleapps.com/

This has improved substantially over time, and now includes a broad range of training for users and administrators.

Google Apps Certified Administrator

http://certification.googleapps.com/admin

This is a nuts-and-bolts certification that ensures you and your IT staff understand the core capabilities in the Admin interface. This certification should be a requirement for everyone with administrative access to your Apps domain.

Part 3: Deploying Ultralight
(A Google Apps Guide)

Ultralight Enablers for Google Apps

Compliance and Security

Vault

https://apps.google.com/products/vault/

Google's own Vault product is included in the pricier Unlimited version of Google Apps. Vault is built to enable regulatory compliance and eDiscovery.

CloudLock

https://www.cloudlock.com/

CloudLock provides Drive encryption, third-party app management, and a variety of policy enforcement tools.

BetterCloud

https://www.bettercloud.com/

BetterCloud combines a number of management, audit, and automated action capabilities into a single tool.

Virtru

https://www.virtru.com/

Virtru enables HIPAA-compliant email encryption, and has begun rolling out file encryption as well.

Backupify

http://www.datto.com/backupify

Now a part of Datto, Backupify pioneered comprehensive cloud-to-cloud backup for Google Apps.

Spanning

http://spanning.com/

Now a part of EMC, Spanning has built a reputation as a powerful and user-friendly backup provider for Google Apps.

Endpoint Management

Google Apps MDM

https://apps.google.com/products/admin/mobile/

Google provides baseline MDM management as part of the Apps package. This includes basic settings for iOS and more robust controls for Android with Android for Work.

JumpCloud

https://jumpcloud.com/

JumpCloud markets itself as a Directory-as-a-Service, extending authentication from Apps to devices through LDAP, RADIUS, or a locally installed client. The client can push custom terminal scripts, turning JumpCloud into a comprehensive management tool for knowledgeable admins.

AirWatch

http://www.air-watch.com/

AirWatch is VMware's very powerful and very complex device and identity management platform. It can manage mobile, Windows and macOS systems, and it includes the kitchen sink besides. It feels as heavy as it is.

MaaS360

http://www-03.ibm.com/security/mobile/maas360.html

A part of IBM, MaaS360 is similar to AirWatch in its ambitions, but with a lighter feature set and feel.

Cisco Meraki

https://meraki.cisco.com/

Meraki makes admins think of networks, not endpoints, but Cisco has built a reporting and mild endpoint management component into Meraki that may be useful in environments with limited requirements.

OneLogin

https://www.onelogin.com/

An identity management solution first, OneLogin has added what they call VLDAP (virtual LDAP) along with client connectors for macOS and Windows. Capabilities are limited to authentication, however, and OneLogin has not shown interest in supporting full blown management.

Samanage

https://www.samanage.com/

Samanage is a passive tool that uses a small client to provide robust reporting into a full-featured asset management and service desk platform. For more active management, it integrates with GoToAssist and LogMeIn.

File Management

AODocs

https://www.aodocs.com/

AODocs plays a vital role making Google Drive capable of operating like a true cloud file server. Not every organization will need what AODocs can do, but for many, AODocs may prove indispensable.

Voice

Dialpad

https://dialpad.com/

Built from the ground up to provide voice services for Google Apps, Dialpad offers a variety of features and smooth integration.

RingCentral

http://www.ringcentral.com/

RingCentral received Google's thumbs up to become one of two recommended voice service (Dialpad being the other).

Grasshopper

http://grasshopper.com/

Ideal for small teams, Grasshopper can take a combination of existing mobile devices and Google Voice and tie them together with a professional PBX-like frontend.

Afterword

This book has spoken to the implications of technology change, particularly the shift from Second Platform to Third Platform thinking. This shift isn't the last time the industry will go through upheaval, and no one can say when the next major disruption will occur.

What does the future look like? What happens when Google Apps for Work becomes a lagging technology? What do we do when the tools that launched us successfully into the cloud start holding us back from what comes next?

First, it is important to remember that the inevitability of change in no way lessens the opportunity facing us today. Moving to the Third Platform starts providing value immediately. The entire model is based on paying for what you need, as you need it – an impossibility in the PC era, where datacenter investments represented five or ten-year commitments.

It does require commitment to a core platform, however, and switching platforms will be non-trivial. The good news is, if it becomes necessary to migrate, the tools are already in place to take ownership of cloud-based data and move it to the next destination.

Google and Microsoft already provide migration tools to move data off their competitor's platform. Backup solutions like Backupify and Spanning, in addition to providing data redundancy, ensure organizational data is accessible even after a core platform relationship is terminated. And API access coupled with custom or third-party tools allow more complex integration and export.

It is impossible to say whether Google Apps and Microsoft Office 365 will evolve to *become* the next thing, or if they'll be completely bypassed by it. In either event, addressing the needs of millions of users on each platform will be a massive business opportunity. And this is probably the best defense we have – in any technological era – against finding ourselves stranded.

Acknowledgements

Nothing in IT is built that isn't built on the efforts and ingenuity of so many we'll never know. We truly stand on the shoulders of giants, and I'm grateful to live in this era of remarkable technological innovation.

Many people helped develop, refine, and support the creation of this book. Many more helped me distill what Ultralight is about, what works, and what doesn't. These wonderful people include members of my immediate family (largely conscripted against their will) as well as Jordan Rice, Ryan Basden, Jordan McCormick, John Wilcoxson, Jerry Goode, Andrew Smith, Eric Sutphen, Alvin Davis, Chip Carnes, and Mike Price.

Jared P. might be horrified to discover he is mentioned here, but our discussion of the role of cloud platforms in business helped plant the seed for this book.

Christine Niles taught me everything I know about editing and publishing, and David Millican helped boil things down into a usable description.

FIN